TRAUMA-SENSITIVE

**A Bible-based guide to teaching children
about bodies, boundaries, and the birds & the bees**

David & Christina,
I don't doubt you're
already incorporating so
much of what I recommend.
Keep up the amazing parenting.
God bless, Geony Rucker

Geony Rucker

©2018 Geony Rucker, Value Unconditional, Inc.

ALL RIGHTS RESERVED
No part of this publication may be reproduced, distributed, or transmitted in any form or by any means, including photocopying, recording, or other electronic or mechanical methods, without the prior written permission of the publisher, except in the case of brief quotations embodied in reviews and certain other non-commercial uses permitted by copyright law.

Printed in the United States of America, The Covington Group, 2018

ISBN Number: 978-0-692-11003-4

Valueunconditional.org

Disclaimer: All names used for illustrative purposes are fictional.

This book is dedicated...

To my spirited little Claire Kamryn,

May God always give me the patience and understanding to answer your questions according to His Word. I love you, Claire Bug!

To my committed and loving Mom Blanca (aka Blanchy) and Dad Floyd (aka Froy) Fisher,

Thank you for always reminding me that I could come to you about anything. No matter how awkward our conversations were—and my goodness gracious were some of them extremely awkward—you still managed to get me to come back and talk to you. Thank you both, so much. You are the most outstanding parents and I'll be forever grateful for the effort you made pouring into my life.

I love you, Mommy and Daddy!

To my husband, Martin T. Rucker II,

Thank you for loving me unconditionally. Thank you for talking to me about grace when I didn't feel I deserved it.
You're a good man, and I'm grateful God picked me for you.

I love you, T!

Contents

Prelude: Little Angel .... *vii*

Parenting Tips for the Talks *1*
    Comfort Levels
    Anatomical Names: Uncomfortable but Necessary
    Starting With a Unanimous Message
    Making Peace with our Past
    Talking Early, Talking Often

Toddlers – 2nd Grade: Setting the stage *17*
    Kid-Set Boundaries
    Body Safety Rules
    Peez, Don't Say Dis

3rd – 5th Grade: My body is… interesting *29*
    Healthy Relationships
    Masturbation
    Sexual Harassment
    Godly Roles vs. Minimizing

6th – 8th Grade: Digging Deeper *45*
    Temptation
    Take Every Thought
    Falling Short
    Honesty is Hard
    8th Grade: Consent and Intoxication

High School: I've been there, honey *71*
    Lines of Communication
    Code Talk
    The 4-1-1
    Options Following Assault
    Identity in Christ

Handling Disclosures, Responding Appropriately & Reporting Abuse *87*

Author's Notes: Application *95*

Prelude: Little Angel

I never expected the produce section of a downtown grocery store would be where I'd finally break. Every ounce of energy had leaked out of me over the previous few months; presentations and paperwork, volunteering and planning a wedding. This was it—I'd reached my limit. I was staring into space—or into mist-covered cucumbers, if you were an onlooker. My eyes were drowning in the memory of the 2nd grader who'd disclosed repeated sexual abuse to me just a few hours prior; I had only the tears streaming down my expressionless, tired face to show for it. It's hard to say how long I stood there. Her gestures were so obvious—her body language cried for help before she ever opened her mouth. When the moment came, my spirit ached with each word she spoke and each movement she made. She'd sluggishly tug at her jacket, fighting back the anxiety of a person with decades of trauma, despite not even yet experiencing a full decade of life.

"I told my mom but she doesn't believe me."

Those words sliced right through me. There could very well have been a tank sitting in the pit of my stomach and I wouldn't have known the difference. I could hear her louder and clearer than the cashier calling for assistance at the customer service counter, or the rush of last-minute shoppers rushing and bustling around me as if they weren't going to be stuck in rush hour traffic regardless. My subconscious questioned whether or not adopting her was reasonable, or legal—my conscious answered with the realization that I was an unmarried twenty-something with little financial stability and an overworked heart. In all the presentations I'd delivered as a community educator for a rape-crisis center, this was by far the most difficult disclosure I'd ever received.

Whether I was in an upper-class private school or an urban-core public school, one thing remained constant: an overwhelming majority of the students did not feel comfortable talking to their parents about sex. Combining that with the never-ending stories of parents who punished their children for asking about sexual phrases or words they'd heard at school or on TV fueled the fury within me. We're suffocating in a world full of sexual content and sinful nature while gasping for encouragement, purity and righteousness. Why is there no counter-argument being delivered through the Christians who proudly praise God every Sunday morning? Why isn't the Word of God being used to attack the deception and manipulation being fed to our children through society's definition of harmless casual sex?

Because parents don't know where to start. We only know what we know. And we fear what we don't know.

Satan has run rampant with wordly, pre-marital, sinful sex for long enough and it is time to give sex back to God. The same God that created the most brilliant hot springs from Oregon to Virginia; the same God that developed an instinctual response to fear, commonly referred to as the "fight, flight or freeze"; He's the same marvelous God that created humans, love and the gifts that come from binding that love into a physical, emotional and spiritual form of expression—we call this fun expression, "sex" and I want you to be so comfortable talking to your kids about it that they're proud to say there's nothing they couldn't ask you. Our God is too good and His Word is too powerful for us to continue to buy Satan's lies of shame.

My prayer is that this Guide will reach church staff and teach them how to present purity in a way that will not only uphold the standard God has set, but also keep survivors of sexual violence from feeling as if they're dirty for having experienced sexual encounters before marriage. I pray this will enable parents with courage, comfort and conversation-starters, to build a stronger relationship with the children in their lives.

Lastly, I pray this Guide will help teach adults how to keep kids safe from the traumas of sexual violence. I have faith that this will help you grow into a more transparent and trusting relationship with your children and spouse. I have faith it will help you internalize God's grace and loving mercy. Thank you for caring about speaking to your child. Thank you for trying to find a way to make those hard conversations a little easier.

Thank you for choosing God's Word as a foundation for teaching kids about sex rather than using the blueprint society has delivered. May God bless you and strengthen you every step of the way...Geony.

Parenting Tips for the Talks

Looking back, it was clear. Parents weren't informed about sexual violence, so they struggled to identify it. They didn't understand its prevalence, so they overlooked disclosures as *crafty imaginations*. When kids asked questions, parents didn't know where to start, so the questions were dismissed and unintentionally outsourced to Google. Those experiences fueled my desire to reach parents. I had to let them in on everything their kids had poured into me but were afraid to share with their own moms and dads. I had to teach them what conversations to have and when to have them. I had to provide adults with a guide, complete with examples of what to say if and when a child ever disclosed sexual abuse. Parents want to keep their kids safe and my experiences can help teach them how to do that. That is how Purity came to be. It combines my love for Jesus and His Word with my relentless determination to educate every living being about the prevalence and dynamics of sexual violence. So, Parents, let's begin...

Every conversation is a building block. You discuss *consent* (defined as honest, happy permission) with 3 and 4-year-olds so that when they get older and the conversation expands, they're already familiar with its application. The building block method keeps the conversations less intimidating for parents and more informal, which kids and parents can both appreciate. I encourage you to think about how to incorporate these different tips into the routines your family already has in place. If you drive Sarah home from Soccer practice on Tuesdays, that could be a good time to chat about what happened at school or practice. If your husband or wife takes Tyler to the gym to play basketball on Thursday nights, maybe that could be a time for casual discussion. Take your time and reach out to God every chance you get. He'll guide you every step of the way.

> ### *Proverbs 22:4-6 (NKJV)*
> *By humility and the fear of the LORD are riches and honor and life. Thorns and snares are in the way of the perverse; He who guards his soul will be far from them. Train up a child in the way he should go, and when he is old he will not depart from it.*

Building Block: *Comfort Levels*

Children feed off our energy. If your boss is on your case all day, when you go to pick your kiddos up from school or daycare, your little one might ask, "what's wrong?" just by seeing the look on your face. If their babysitter gets in a fight with her boyfriend, it doesn't matter how badly she tries to hold it together, our kids will sense something is off. If grandma doesn't feel good, kiddos pick up on it. Perhaps it's their purity. We could consider it *kid's intuition*, if you will. Whatever we want to call it—they're onto us.

This is why we have to address our own discomfort before starting these tough conversations with the kids in our lives. Know that it's also okay to tell your children that this conversation isn't easy on you because perhaps the person who had this discussion with you when you were little, didn't have the conversation quite the way that you want to have it with your children; perhaps as a child, you didn't have this conversation *at all*. Addressing that it is a tough conversation for you doesn't automatically ruin "the vibe" so long as you are calmly making an effort to continue the conversation. They need to know that you feeling a little uncomfortable doesn't mean they're in trouble or that they're "being bad" for talking about this with you. They need to feel like they can come to you and ask absolutely ANY-

THING; vulnerability and transparency set the stage for open communication and that begins with you. While you may be embarrassed about it as your babies get older, conversations get deeper, and questions get more provocative, honesty remains the necessary policy. My parents always felt uncomfortable, but by golly they made sure I knew they were always there for me. It is your job to keep your kids open and willing to ask questions.

The adult sets the level of comfort. To help you, there are some easy and applicable ways we can create a more comfortable environment for these conversations.

1. Give me snacks or give me silence! I can't possibly be the only person who appreciates snacks. I'll talk to you about anything you want if you set some Flaming Hot Cheetos down in front of me. My dad will sit in a room for hours with you if you have food of any kind. Our little ones are the same way! Food is social and simple. Instead of doing a snack that they can grab and walk away with (like half of a PB&J), have something small enough that they *want* to stick around. Grapes, Cheez-Its, trail mix. Chit chat with them about their day and create a sense of normalcy in having casual conversations. Not every conversation is going to be super deep, but if you normalize discussion, it makes those deep conversations that much easier. Bringing snacks along for the ride home from school might mean having pretzel crumbs in your carpet, but it's also likely to pull your child's guard down. I encourage food. Anyone who knows me is not surprised the first tip involves eating. Bon Appétit!

2. Normalize Deep Discussion. We usually have only a few years of opportunity where our kiddos think we are just the absolute coolest. This eventually turns into thinking parents couldn't possibly be more embarrassing. If at all possible, catch 'em while you're still on their "cool" list. This is a time when they really care about your opinion, so they ask you questions about any and everything: Why is the sky blue? How do worms breathe underground? Why do dogs have hair everywhere and humans don't? In these moments, feel free to open the door to deeper discussion. Ask them what issues they would solve if they became president. If your kid still thinks you're cool, they're probably 7 or younger. This means their answers are going to be pretty ridiculous. When our babies have irrational answers, it doesn't matter if we are trying to create an environment where they feel comfortable speaking to us—we should encourage their imaginations. "If you were president you would do what?! You'd give free crayons to everyone?! Wow! That's a great idea! How would you get to people who live deep in the mountains?!" We want our little ones to grow up feeling like they can tell us what is honestly on their mind. It may seem trivial when the subject is crayon distribution, but you'll be grateful for this foundation as the topics intensify.

Note: If you little ones aren't so little anymore, hope is not lost. You haven't missed your opportunity. We'll talk more about the older stages as we get further into the guide. This information is still important for you to know.

Building Block: *Fight the Urge: Asking Before Advising*

As parents we want so unbelievably badly to guide and advise, guide and advise, guide and advise . . . When the issues are, "Mom, dis banana won't open!," then openly giving direction is fine. Unfortunately, as the issues turn into those drama-filled Junior High years, our kids will often just want us to *listen*. Listen to how they're feeling. Listen to their hurts. Validate their emotions and pay attention. The listening is what will build trust and increase the likelihood of their asking you questions or leaning on you for advice. It gives them an opportunity to express what's on their mind without feeling judged or shut down. The issue with advising isn't necessarily with *giving advice*, but rather that we often give it *too early*. They're venting, at the peak of their frustration, and we butt-in with, "Just don't talk to her anymore if she's going to be mean to you" while simultaneously finishing dinner and putting the dishes away. That response not only makes them think you don't understand them (because you'd never respond that way if you did, *duh mom*) but it also tells them that what they're feeling and thinking about the situation isn't nearly as important to you as finding a solution. They don't see how much you have going on and frankly, they're kids, they don't care.

What they care about is that someone did something that they found completely unacceptable. We have to *listen*. Know whether it was Ana or Stephanie that was flirting with Ryan and which one sent the mean text. If they're repeatedly saying how angry they are, help them identify the underlying emotion, as anger is often preceded by feeling frustrated, jealous, left out, betrayed or insulted. Anger is the emotion we claim to be experiencing when we're too proud to vulnerably admit someone hurt our feelings. This is keeping the focus on what they're feeling and will make them feel like it's important to you, too. Mastering how to identify what emotions we're feeling is healthy and can help us communicate more effectively in our relationships. Imagine how much easier it will be to find a solution if we're able to identify precisely what is bothering or hurting us. That is a good tool to teach your children early on.

When their voice is no longer raised, and hand gestures lose their previous tension, you know they're coming off of their *peak*. Find an appropriate moment and then ask if they want to know your advice.

"Well sugar bug, do you want to know what I think?"

"Oh (insert your own cute pet name here), I'm so sorry you're dealing with that. That is so frustrating... Do you want my advice?"

If the situation can put them or someone else in a harmful situation, then we definitely want to give them advice and ensure everyone is kept safe. Ask God for wisdom, clarity, and discernment as you navigate the waters of those conversations. Also, don't be too hard on yourself. You've only got so much patience and some days, you might not be able to hold space. It's okay to have your spouse step in. This is trial and error, folks! It's building a foundation for an open, transparent relationship and that takes time. You have everything it takes to create strong, lasting relationships with your babies. If you didn't, God wouldn't have placed them in your care.

> *Ephesians 1:17-18 (NKJV)*
> *... that the God of our Lord Jesus Christ, the Father of glory, may give to you a spirit of wisdom and of revelation in the knowledge of Him. I pray that the eyes of your heart may be enlightened, so that you will know what is the hope of His calling, what are the riches of the glory of His inheritance in the saints.*

Building Block: *Anatomical Names: Uncomfortable but Necessary*

"Wee wee, muffin, ding ding, monkey, va-jay-jay, hoo haw, thingy" . . . we come up with all sorts of oddly creative things to avoid saying penis or vagina. Why do we do that?! Because at some point in our lives, someone made us feel like saying those words is inappropriate and uncomfortable. We don't teach kids nicknames for their chins, ankles or eyebrows, so as they grow up, they talk about these parts of their bodies without any shame or hesitation. We need to create the same safe environment for the private parts of their bodies. There are many reasons for this.

First, I can assure you that there is no part of God that wants us to believe there is an atom in our body that is shameful or dirty. Secondly, as children develop, they grow through a variety of stages. When they're in those early years between 3 and 5 (ish), they are extremely curious about bodies and bodily functions. They're more interested in peeking when people are changing or trying to watch when someone is going to the bathroom. If we openly talk about the things on their mind, including those funny penises and vaginas, or why grown-up women have *boobies* but little girls don't, they're going be more likely to come to us when kids mention these private parts on the playground or at daycare.

Secondly, having the correct anatomical names can also be helpful through the early childhood development as most children go through a stage where they enjoy being completely (or nearly) naked. The "wanna-be-nakey" stage usually strikes around 2 or 3. This is normal. So what do you do if you have a 3-year-old boy and a 7-year-old girl, or visa versa? You tell them the truth long before they realize it on their own: boys and girls have different parts. "A boy goes tinkle through a penis and a girl goes tinkle through a vagina, and we all poop through our bottoms" – then mentally prepare for laughter and lots of talk about poop. Discussing bodily functions is also developmental and completely normal, so no shame in that. By having a no-judgment, no-shame approach in teaching your kids that they potty differently, you're avoiding any awkward confusion when one of your kids hits that weird "I'm gonna go ahead and strip naked in the center of the living room" stage right in front of their opposite-sex sibling.

Much less amusing than the bodily-function obsessed toddlers is the third reason we want to use anatomical names: child-sexual abuse affects roughly 1 in 4 girls and 1 in 6 boys before they reach their 18th birthday (http://nctsn.org/nctsn_assets/pdfs/caring/ChildSexualAbuseFactSheet.pdf). When a child attempts to disclose an experience to a safe adult, we want to ensure the adults in his or her life knows what the child is trying to communicate. Using anatomical terminology will be more likely to catch an adult's attention than nicknames. If a child comes up to their teacher and says, "Mr.Richard touched my muffin after dinner!" the adult will most likely respond with something close to, "That's nice honey, please go back to your seat." If a child comes up and says, "Mr.Richard touched my penis (or vagina) after dinner," that teacher will, hopefully, take the appropriate steps necessary as a mandated reporter, beginning with, "I'm so sorry that happened to you, (insert child's name). I believe you. That was so brave of you to tell a safe grown up! Thank you for telling me."

Using the correct anatomical names for those parts of our bodies increases the likelihood that our children will feel comfortable sharing questions with us (instead of google) and will help them embrace that they are perfect just as God created them. There is no part of their being that they need to feel shame or embarrassment about. We want them to know that they are fearfully and wonderfully made, and that doesn't just mean certain parts of them. Every square inch of their entire being is perfect just how God made it.

> *Psalm 139:14 (NIV)*
> *I praise you because I am fearfully and wonderfully made; your works are wonderful, I know that full well*

Building Block: *Start with a Unanimous Message*

When I was in Junior High, a letter went out to parents that Ms. Lopez, my P.E. teacher, was going to be be teaching the 8th grade girls about "health" and the male P.E. teacher would be speaking to the 8th grade boys about the same. We would be held in different rooms to have an educational discussion about our bodies and *the changes* we were facing. We were all horrified and wondered what Ms. Lopez was going to teach us that we didn't already know. Many of us also wanted to know what the boys were going to be covering. What were they learning that was so different from what we were learning? As an adult I fully understand why a school or church would separate boys and girls to discuss puberty and all the fun pimples and hair that accompany this process. I was also grateful that we were separated back then, as were the rest of the Junior High girls. Seeing your crush on the other side of the room while the teacher talks about tampons would be enough horror to fake sick for weeks!

While puberty is a completely understandable topic for a school or church to host separately and deliver separate messages, when it comes to purity, the boys and girls need to be hearing the exact same message. There is an unhealthy and manipulated message in our culture that says girls must never allow themselves to be touched while telling boys they are awesome if they manage to touch lots of girls. I love America with my whole heart, but by golly it would make my life much easier if the culture didn't teach our kids the things it does. There is a message that says boys get "urges" and girls are just urged for. This is destructive on many levels and is light-years from being Biblically based. Both boys and girls deserve an age-appropriate understanding that both genders are called to the same sexual expectation. There isn't a boys Bible and a girls Bible when it comes to sex. We all got the same Bible, and we're all called to the same sexual standards. If we hold our girls to the Biblical standard of waiting until marriage but imply to our boys that it's not a huge deal if they do the same, whether or not it's our intention, we're teaching them that the standard set in our culture is superior to the standard set in the Word of God. Our boys deserve better. Our boys deserve to know the urges American culture tells them are too strong to ignore is manipulation of the enemy. We are fearfully and wonderfully made and boys are included. God did not instill in us desires too strong for our own will power, but how often are boys reminded of that? It's our job to teach both genders that "urges" are experienced by both genders, are 100% natural and normal and are part of the biology God used to create us, and there is no shame in this. Girls often need to hear this aspect so they don't internalize guilt or shame when they start to notice the guy on that cologne commercial that has big muscles and just flipped some sort of internal switch ON. It doesn't mean they're dirty because they have hormones, but sometimes it feels that way if you're told that boys are the only ones with urges. Girl hormones do more than just try to make them irritable once a month, and we'll discuss that more as we cover puberty. Most importantly, when it comes to teaching purity, our kids need to understand the context of why those urges and hormones were created.

The message will grow almost as quickly as our babies do, but one of the best things you can do for your daughter or son is to ensure they are always receiving the same Biblical message as the opposite-sex.

> ### 1 Corinthians 10:12-13 (NIV)
> *So, if you think you are standing firm, be careful that you don't fall! No temptation has overtaken you except what is common to mankind. And God is faithful; he will not let you be tempted beyond what you can bear. But when you are tempted, he will also provide a way out so that you can endure it.*

Building Block: *Making Peace with Our Past*

If you have made it this far without feeling at least a teeny bit uncomfortable, you were probably either raised by an OB/GYN or a social worker. Before we dive into making peace with our own past, let's scratch down a few things to help ease into the discussion:

Did an adult have "the talk" with you growing up? If so, write a few of the details below. How did you feel about the discussion?

_____

_____

_____

_____

What were some things they said that you'd like to pass on (or avoid passing on) to your own children?

_____

_____

_____

_____

What social, spiritual or familial influences do you think made you view sex and purity the way you do?

_____

_____

_____

_____

Whoever taught you about fruit salad did so in such a way that you don't feel anxiety when discussing it. You can talk about many kinds of fruits and even vegetables without feeling your stomach drop down to your knees. If you don't feel the same way talking about sex, the "why" is probably up in those answers your just wrote down. If not in those answers, it's in the environment you witnessed growing up at school, church and society's view on sex.

I was in Kindergarten when a boy in my class came up to me on the playground as asked me if I wanted to have sex with him. "What's that?" I responded. "It's when you kiss and hug with no clothes on! My cousins and I pretend to do it all the time!" he said enthusiastically. As a sexual violence educator, I now look back at this situation and see the likely abuse that was taking place in his home. As many as 93 percent of victims under the age of 18 know their abuser, so hearing that it was cousins does not in any way make me believe it wasn't abuse (https://www.rainn.

org/statistics/children-and-teens). Well, my 5-year-old self ended up shouting, "EW! NO! I DON'T WANT TO HAVE SEX WITH *YOU*! I WANT TO HAVE SEX WITH . . ." and before I know it I'm being pulled into the principal's office. A phone call from my christian school sending me home for yelling about who I wanted to pursue sexually wasn't concerning to my parents at all, I'm sure.

Sarcasm

...And that is how we ended up having to talk about sex.

As an only child, any serious "family discussion" is a little intimidating because you know it's about you. My poor mom was devastated. "You're just a baby ... you shouldn't know about this" was a line I heard many times that day. As a survivor of significant childhood trauma, she didn't have a clue what a 5-year-old was supposed to know; she struggled to even find the place to redirect our conversation. She thought she had years before I asked tough questions. Blanchy (my mom's name is Blanca but my dad nicknamed her Blanch and it stuck) was sitting on the side of her bed. Her eyes were pacing left to right while she tried to find the words to say; "That's all he said, right? Just kissing and hugging with no clothes on?" She had to have asked that at least 25 times. I was ashamed because I knew I did something really terrible if it made my school send me home, but I also wanted to comfort my mom because she looked upset. I was confused, but definitely curious. I had to be in trouble, right? Is it because sex means you're naked? They knew I wasn't going to actually get naked on the playground, right? All I ended up finding out from her that day is that boys and girls have "different parts." She'd pulled out a medical level anatomy book to start by explaining the girl part and that its name is, "vagina." She couldn't muster up the strength to turn to the boy page, and despite my efforts, I didn't know the boy part name or what it looked like, so my flipping through pages looking for it did me no good.

I'm not the only person who had an experience as a child where they realized sexual stuff, penises and vaginas are embarrassing or not to be discussed. On a short-term level, not having awkward conversations keeps us feeling more comfortable. Postponing conversations makes us feel like we're protecting them or sheltering them from the sin that's overtaken our world. Sometimes postponing conversations makes us think maybe they'll forget about the discussion and then we don't have to talk about it until another knucklehead brings it up. Realistically, by avoiding these conversations, we are putting our children in unsafe positions where their vulnerability can be exploited by the resources which are very willing to answer their questions without regard of God's Word—those being people *or* the internet.

Building Block: *Talking Early, Talking Often*

Incorporating these discussions into casual conversation is the best protocol. The earlier you begin letting your children know they can come to you with questions of any kind, the easier it will be to bounce off of that solid foundation. You want to be where they turn when they have questions. Google is a brilliant tool that if used the wrong way, can expose our babies to sexual immorality, pornography and even conversations with people looking to harm them. By talking early and talking often, we are doing our part in keeping our kids safe. More importantly, we are embracing the responsibility God gave us when he blessed us with our little ones. You have been entrusted with your children because you have what it takes to raise them up according to His will. If you were meant to have your co-worker's little angel kids, you would have. Your children are yours because you have the gifts, strengths and tools they specifically need to grow according to His word. You can try to step halfway into that role, but just like stepping halfway into the shower, it's not going to get the job done.

Part of communicating with them is recognizing our role vs God's role. Parents always want to be able to tell kids, "I promise I'll never let anything happen to you." Is that really fair to say? Is it true? No. You can't be everywhere they are at all times. It also puts them in a tough situation because if and when anything *does* happen to them, they wonder why you didn't keep them safe. Now they're wondering, perhaps on a subconscious level, "if you said you can keep me safe and you couldn't, then what else have you told me that I actually can't trust you about?" That might also lead to an unfair amount of guilt that parents carry because they feel they let their child down by not protecting them. How completely unreasonable is that?!

Instead of making big, bold promises that we can never uphold, consider saying, "I promise to always believe you when you tell me something," "I promise to always have your back," "I promise that even when you do something wrong, I'll be here for you" or "I promise to always do my best to help you achieve your dreams." Tell them what is true and what you can uphold.

God's role is different. His promises are big and bold and we can always trust and rely on the power of His Word. He can be everywhere we are at all times. He has sent the Holy Spirit to be our healer, comforter and advocate in place of Jesus living among us here on earth (John 14:26). Even when we are alone, we can call upon him for strength (Isaiah 41:10). Does loving and obeying God mean that nothing bad will ever happen to us? No. God wanting us to choose him rather than being forced to follow him means that we have free will; not everyone uses their free will for good and sometimes that results in bad things happening to good people. It's extremely difficult to understand why good things happen to bad people, so sometimes we'll try to force ourselves into believing that people get what they deserve—good things happen to good people and bad things happen to bad people. Fortunately, there is an old guy named Job that we can read about in the bible. He was a blameless man. He was great at avoiding evil, but reading about His life can show us what it looks like when a whole bunch of bad stuff happens to a really good person. He remained faithful to God and God provided in the long run. The best thing we can do for our children is raise them up to know and understand who God the Father is. The guidance of the Holy Spirit can keep them on the right path with far more patience and grace than any human parent could ever contain. This is all possible because of Jesus. Our children have to understand the foundation so these discussions make sense as they get older.

> **Stand on these promises God has made us:**
> *I'll give you a way out when you're tempted* (1 Corinthians 10:13)
> *I hear your cry* (Psalms 34:17; Psalm 118)
> *You have no reason to fear* (Isaiah 41:10-16; Psalms 27:1)
> *You can be filled with the Holy Spirit* (Psalms 1:23)
> *Everyone can have the gift of prophecy* (Acts 2:17)
> *You can be forgiven* (2 Corinthians 7:14; 1 John 1:9)
> *I will guide and direct you* (Psalm 32:8; Proverbs 3:5,6)

What a blessing that out of every person on the planet, God thought of you and your spouse and said, "I have the perfect child for these two individuals." Do you realize the depth in that? He can think of you and not only tell you your full name (spelled correctly), but he can also blurt out your likes, dislikes, deepest secrets, biggest regrets, things you're allergic to and the people you *wish* were allergic to you—all without hesitation. More importantly, he knows the destiny and purpose he has in store for your life (Jeremiah 29:11). He knows the gifts that will come into fruition if you align yourself with His Word, and that's such a big part of the reason why he's cheering you on in every step of your life's journey. His knowledge far surpasses our understanding, so it can be difficult to understand the fullness of His plan for us or the purpose of different things we face.

Our thoughts are not His thoughts and our ways are not His ways (Isaiah 55:8-9). Part of God's plan for you is those precious kids in your life (biological or not) who are the focus of this guide and why you are reading it. Whether they're in your life for just a season (shout out to all the youth pastors, teachers and foster parents reading this book) or whether you're stuck with them for life (shout out to all the families of children), God has placed them in your path for a purpose. You have everything it takes to raise them up to fulfill the calling He has on their lives. Maybe you didn't have somebody set a good example and now you're doing your best to do better for your kids. Maybe your parents were fantastic and you wonder if you could measure up. Either way, I can assure you that there are gifts within you that you haven't even tapped into yet. You have abilities through Christ that you've not yet realized or accepted and it's my prayer that you throw away the bungee cord and dive in full-throttle, in anticipation for him to catch you with grace-filled, merciful, widespread, loving arms. What better example can we be for our children than to reflect the relationship God shares with us as our Heavenly Father?

Toddlers – 2nd Grade

Beyond the marker-stained hands and velcro-strapped shoes there's a little spirit, undeniably formed by God. They don't always act like it—sometimes they're little heathens—but there's no doubt they were created by God. So many creative ideas, so little filters. We want to do what we can to protect their innocence and sweet purity; we also want them to know what they can do to keep themselves safe.

This is the age range where we start talking about our bodies and boundaries. They do a lot to help start the conversation, too! When kids are in this stage of development, they are very curious about bodies. They might try to catch you changing or even peek while people are going to the bathroom. Having a thorough understanding of what is normal and what is concerning is important as we help mold them into respectful little humans. We don't have to wait to tell our children the appropriate anatomical terms for their body parts. They can learn whether or not they have a penis or vagina as they learn about every other part of their body. This means they'll probably know these words around 2 years old. This will be far harder on you than it will be on them. You feel weird about it because you've been taught to feel weird about it. Your child knowing the names of private parts does not mean they have lost their innocence. They will only know it's weird or uncomfortable if you make them feel like it's weird or uncomfortable. A great time to bring it up is when talking about "tinkling" a.k.a urinating. My daughter was 5 months old the first time I said, "And you know what's a funny difference between boys and girls? They tinkle differently! That's because boys have a penis and girls have a vagina. But you're still a little tinkle monster! You're my pretty little tinkle monster!" because she has what feels like 4,000 wet diapers a day. We had this chat while I changed her diaper and filled her in on my friend Gina who had just had a baby boy. I explained that the way doctors know if a baby is a boy or a girl is all based on whether they have a penis or a vagina. Will she remember that conversation? Nope. Probably not. But the earlier I start using those words around her (in the safe context of tinkling) the less she'll learn to associate them as being shameful.

Building Block: *Kid-Set Boundaries*

We all have that cheek-pinching, gently waddling "Aunt Marsha" regularly invading our personal space. She's super touchy feely. She has that gentle, under-her-breath giggle and whips it out even during casual conversation when there isn't really anything funny going on. Not sure who she is in your family? Ask your kids. They know because she tries hugging and snuggling them far more than she tries snuggling and hugging adults. Kids are loveable and we like to make them happy. Makes sense. No harm, no foul.

However...

Those hugs and snuggles and cheek-pinches are only going to make the kid feel loved and happy if they *want* to be hugged, snuggled or pinched. It's a horrible example of us as parents if our kids are impolite or disrespectful so we often teach our children to use their manners and greet guests/hosts accordingly. We do need to make sure, though, that we are respecting their boundaries and giving them a say in how they feel comfortable greeting. Our children need to know that if for whatever reason they don't feel comfortable shaking hands, hugging or kissing someone, you will have their back and support them as they politely decline. Touches of any kind should never be forced. To ensure we're maintaining a mannerly disposition, it's okay to tell them they should acknowledge each guest with a wave-and-name combo. "Hello Mr. Anderson" combined with eye contact and those flappy little fingers is just as polite as awkwardly pressing your body up against somebody that you don't feel like touching.

When we force our kids to hug people that they don't want to hug (ourselves included) we're teaching them that their consent doesn't matter when it comes to grown-ups. We're showing them that they don't have say over their own body. We're teaching them that because a grown-up wants to touch them, even if the kid doesn't want them to, they have to let them because that person's a grown up. Even if it isn't our intention, that's a very dangerous mentality to give our children. We hate to think we could play any role in making our children more vulnerable because if given a direct decision, we'd choose their safety 1,000 times over. Yet what we know is that children view adults as authoritative figures. When authoritative figures ask them to put their plate in the sink, they know they should do so. When the teacher tells them it's time to come in from recess, they know they should come in *or there will be consequences*. When we associate touches as just another category of things they're required to do if an adult or older family member asks them to, they feel far more pressured to comply. However, if we tell our kids that they never have to touch anyone or let anyone touch them if they don't want to, and that no matter what, we'll support them, we're giving them a sense of security and support to fall back on. We're also creating the foundation for the "consent" conversation, which will expand exponentially by the time they reach High School.

The more we learn about childhood sexual abuse and the way children respond to trauma, the more we know our children need us to let them know we trust their judgment of people and support their decisions to wave instead of kiss or hug when they feel uncomfortable. A great way to incorporate kid-set boundaries in this age is stop-and-go tickles. Hearing our little ones laugh is probably greater medicine than our own laughter, and what better way to get them to laugh than by tickling them, right?! Well, this is only a great way to make them laugh if they *want* to be tickled. Laughter doesn't mean they want to be tickled and laughter is not consent. Laughter from tickling is nothing more than your body responding to a stimulus. I know that sounds ridiculous but sure enough, God was really cool about how he made us. Our bodies were made to respond to stimuli, whether mental or physical. That's why our mouth waters just thinking about taking a big bite into a sour, juicy lemon. This is why we jump if we hear an unexpected firework. Even babies jump if a loud noise startles them! Researchers at the University of Tuebingen in Germany analyzed what parts of the brain responded when their test subjects heard a funny joke vs when they were tickled. Unlike when hearing a joke, when being tickled, there was activity in the hypothalamus. They stated, "This is the area of the brain that triggers the primitive desire to flee danger" and "the researchers believe the activation of the hypothalamus indicates that our response to tickling may be a primitive defense mechanism to signal submissiveness in the face of a dominating foe."

(http://bigthink.com/robby-berman/why-we-may-love-to-tickle-but-we-mostly-hate-to-be-tickled-ourselves)

If you're a science nerd, definitely check out the study. You'll enjoy it! Stop-and-go tickles empower your child to give you verbal permission when to tickle them and when to stop. This makes tickles far more enjoyable and reinforces the mentality that they pick who touches them and when they are touched. The game itself actually instigates more laughter because of the suspense of when they're going to say, "Okay, tickle me!" Feel free to dramatically pull your hands back with an outlandish noise upon their, "Stop!" command for extra giggles.

Aaaaand You're Naked Again...

You look away for 3.5 seconds and your toddler is naked... again. Maybe they take their pants off and watch TV or strip naked and try to play in the sink water. Do not be concerned. This is a very normal stage. Kids go through a funny little rebellion against clothing before they start recognizing what is meant to be public and what is meant to be private. If our little ones try getting naked in public, we don't want to embarrass them. Instead, let's explain to them that they're only allowed to be naked in their bedrooms or in the bathroom before hopping in the bath. You can use the *bathing suit rule* which essentially tells your children that if you have to cover it up in the swimming pool, it has to be covered up when hanging out at home.

Let's be mindful of the way we communicate the rules so they don't feel shamed. It's completely normal to want to be naked and to go through the naked toddler stage. We don't want them to feel bad about such a natural part of their development.

This is also the age range where they start realizing their body feels different depending on where they touch it. Sometimes toddlers will even start sleeping with their hands in their pants. This is normal. This is another natural part of their development that we don't want them to feel ashamed about. If we think about how much stuff they've learned just in their short life, it makes sense why they want to explore their bodies! They know how pizza tastes and are familiar with the rush of going down a water slide. When things seem new, they want to investigate. A healthy response to your child touching, rubbing, poking or looking at the private parts of their body is to let them know that if they have questions they can ask you, but private parts of our body aren't supposed to be inspected in public. Angela Oswalt, MSW suggests the best practice for parents and caregivers in these uncomfortable situations is to guide children towards more socially appropriate behavior to get the children to refocus without shaming them in the process. (http://wyo-mentalhealth.org/poc/view_doc.php?type=doc&id=10119&cn=461)

It's also important to discuss personal boundaries and let them know that nobody is allowed to see or touch the private parts of their body. They should also know that they aren't allowed to see or touch the private parts of anyone else's body, either. If your child is "playing doctor" with another child the same age (or very close in age) and looking at each other's privates, that can be a normal curiosity. However, there are some key indicators that help identify what is a natural curiosity and what should be concerning. If the age gap is a 5-year-old and an 8-year-old, I would be concerned. The National Child Traumatic Stress Network published an outstanding guide for parents and caregivers on sexual development in young children. They explain:

"Most sexual play is an expression of children's natural curiosity and should not be a cause for concern or alarm. In general, "typical" childhood sexual play and exploration:

- Occurs between children who play together regularly and know each other well
- Occurs between children of the same general age and physical size
- Is spontaneous and unplanned
- Is infrequent
- Is voluntary (the children agreed to the behavior, none of the involved children seem uncomfortable or upset)
- Is easily diverted when parents tell children to stop and explain privacy rules

Some childhood sexual behaviors indicate more than harmless curiosity, and are considered sexual behavior problems." (2 http://nctsn.org/nctsn_assets/pdfs/caring/sexualdevelopmentandbehavior.pdf)

Body Safety Rules

So before the Purity presentations and book writing, I actually worked at a rape crisis center. One of my roles there was doing community education in classrooms for elementary kiddos. While Pre-K received a more delicate version than 4th grade, they all learn the same big picture: these are the important basics of what to do if anyone ever tries to look at, or touch, the private parts of our bodies. I made sure the children knew three important rules: say no, get away and tell someone.

In my experience, saying the rules with British or Jamaican accents made the kids more likely to shout them out and remember them, too. What is so important for the kids to learn is that even if they don't say *no*, and even if they can't get away, it's still not their fault and they should still always tell someone. As Christian parents, we understand that God delicately wove us together in the womb. We understand we were carefully made, but sometimes we overlook how early His brilliant precision shines through. We're given instinctual fight, flight or freeze responses visible even in very young kiddos. As much as we would want to be angry at our children for "allowing" any abuse or assault to take place, we truly have to take a step back and recognize their inability to overpower God-given, instinctual responses. Even as adults we're unable to overrule these predispositions. I'm referring to fight, flight or freeze responses when talking about predispositions. When God made us, he gave our body a "fire alarm" of sorts, to set off a siren when we are in danger. This alarm is called an amygdala and it is located in the brain. What's interesting is that the alarm goes off whether we are in actual danger or simply perceived danger. That's why when we watch scary movies, even though we know we are not in actual danger, we still experience an accelerated heart rate and muscle tension. We can't fault our kids for whatever their God-given instinctual responses are. It's because of this that we want children to know that even if they are too scared to say no (fight), and even if they're too scared to run away (flight), it's still not their fault (duh) and they should still always tell someone.

Explain to them that while touches should never be forced, they should also never be secrets. That's why we always want to tell a safe grown-up if someone tries to get us to keep a touch a secret. The child may also be afraid if the person is older or bigger than them. Their response to someone trying to exploit their vulnerabilities is not the reason something happens to them. If nobody tried to do something in the first place, their response would be irrelevant. It is always the fault of the perpetrator, regardless of the age of the victim.

We've heard of "good touches" and "bad touches." But we're really missing a key part if we only mention those two. Let's always teach our kids about *confusing* touches, too.

Good Touch: This type of touch is safe, wanted by both recipient and distributor, and makes us feel happy.

Examples: **Hugs, Pat on the back, high-five** *Keep in mind, your kid has to want the hug, pat on the back or high-five for it to be considered a good touch*

Bad Touch: This type of touch is unsafe and makes us sad or mad. This type of touch physically hurts us.

Examples: **Kick, punch, slap, pinch**

Confusing Touch: This type of touch might not hurt like a bad touch, but it's definitely not safe like a good touch. It might make us feel weird, confused or maybe even a little sad. A confusing touch is a touch to the private parts of our body for no good reason. There are only two good reasons for people to ever have to touch or see the private parts of our body and those are to keep us clean (diaper changes, for example) or to keep us healthy (doctors doing an exam).

Examples: Anyone trying to **touch or see private parts** of the body, anyone trying to **expose themselves**, anyone introducing **images or videos where private parts of the body are seen.**

This is where the **5-Person Rule** comes into play! Our kids, whether they're 5 years old or 65 years old, should always have 5 safe grown ups they'd feel comfortable telling if anyone ever tried to touch or see the private parts of their body or tried to expose themselves to the child. Why does a 65 year old need to have safe grown ups? Well, trauma impacts the brain in some pretty difficult ways. If someone is assaulted, regardless of their age, they'd be far better off to already have a plan in place of who they'd tell in that situation than to wait for it to happen to make those decisions. It's sometimes difficult to identify assault after it takes place because our mind protects us with denial. What thoughts make sense to our non-traumatized mind may not be as easy to reach with a mind recovering from mental, emotional or even physical distress. Have your kids, family and friends come up with 5 people they'd feel comfortable telling if and when someone ever made them feel uncomfortable or sexually assaulted them. When you ask young kids about who they would tell, don't be surprised if they respond with the name of a pet. We want to ensure we don't make them feel silly when they're sharing this with us. They're being vulnerable and open by telling us who makes them feel safe. Let's encourage that transparency.

Here is an idea for how to respond if your child names a pet:

Parent: "Can you think of anyone you'd tell if someone ever tried to see or touch the private parts of your body?"

Kid: "Ummmm... I'd tell... Mittins!! Mittins, the cat!"

Parent: "Mittins is a great listener! But . . . Mittins probably couldn't do very much to keep you safe, huh? If you want to tell Mittins, you can. But let's think of a safe human grown up who might be able to do more to help. Can you think of anyone else?"

Who are some grown ups you'll recommend to your children if they're having trouble thinking of someone?

1._____

2._____

3._____

4._____

5._____

Mom or Dad, You probably won't make that list of 5 people. That is okay and completely normal!! This does not mean you're a bad parent or that your kids don't trust you. Kids don't want to let their parents down or make them sad. Thinking about telling parents something that will hurt their feelings isn't appealing. To make it tougher, kids are often afraid that they did something wrong to make this happen and they're afraid they'll get in trouble. So long as your child is telling a safe grown-up, you're in a great position. That means we want to ensure the friends and friends' parents in our babies lives are informed on this topic like we are. We also want to teach our kids how to handle disclosures in the event that they end up being the "safe person" to someone else at some point in their lives.

As your kids grow older, you can discuss what the discomfort might include in further detail. While a young kiddo might be referring to Grandma who always forces hugs or kisses, a 5th grader might reference someone snapping their bra in class or slapping their butt. Your junior high student might be talking about someone trying to show them pornographic images or videos at recess—yes, this happens in Junior high—we actually warn parents about this as early as 7 or 8-years-old. In High School we want to discuss this in terms of sexual violence and rape. Handling disclosures with grace, patience and compassion can truly be the launch into the healing survivors need.

Peez Don't Say Dis...

There are many things you'll hear parents say when kids are in this age range. A few of them are, "boys will be boys," "he/she picks on you cause he/she likes you!" and, "oh, kids just say the darndest things."

These leave an impression on the kids who hear them. What do we mean when we say "boys will be boys?" The American culture we discussed earlier on heavily influences this statement. Boys will be boys is not biblical, I can assure you. Boys will uphold the standard set for them and will try to get away with what they believe they can get away with—just like girls. If we give them a way out by saying, "Welp, guess there's not much I can do. He's just a boy!" we're wholeheartedly accepting the enemy's manipulation. God has set the standard for us—boys included.

The things we're saying and teaching our kids when they're tiny, little sponges create the foundation that everything else in their lives is built. While saying, "he/she picks on you cause he/she likes you!" may seem harmless and trivial, we're teaching them to overlook or even accept when someone hurts them, teases them, or does something they may not appreciate, simply because that person likes them. Rather than communicating that this is a sign of affection, let's work on teaching our children how to address situations that make them uncomfortable. This may even include responding to adults making the statement, "he/she is doing it cause he/she likes you!"

A few simple, respectful responses are:

- "I know you feel like they're doing this because they like me but I don't like it. Please make them stop."
- "I don't like being pinched (poked, chased, etc) even if they do like me. Please make them stop."

> ***Proverbs 31:8-9 (NASB)***
> *Open your mouth for the mute, for the rights of all the unfortunate. Open your mouth, judge righteously, and defend the rights of the afflicted and needy.*

Kids might pretend that a dinosaur jumped through the TV and drank all the soda in the refrigerator. Kids might make up a story that a fairy princess appeared in their room and sprinkled glitter into the carpet. Kids do not make up stories about sexual violence. Their imagination doesn't know how to create adult situations. If your child is familiar with adult situations and describing them with child language, it's because they've been exposed to something (or someone) that has shown them what it is. Keep this in mind if and when you hear a friend or coworker dismiss something a child is showing concern about.

3rd – 5th Grade: My body is… interesting

*E*ight is too late. That's the running motto in anti-sexual violence world. Eight's too late. If you haven't talked to your kid about sex by the time they're eight, they've already heard about it on the playground. They might not call it "sex" and they might not have asked you about it, but they're hearing about it. Christian school, Catholic school, public school, border school, charter school, culinary school—doesn't matter.

Visualize their minds as little dry-erase boards. If you get a brand new board, whatever you write on there is going to show up and it's going to look fabulous. But let's pretend you scribble and draw and play a whole bunch of tic-tac-toe on said board. When you go to erase it, you'll get the majority off, but there may still be a tint of that messy, red marker you used. When the next person goes to write on it, and let's say they try to use a green marker, it doesn't matter how attractive the green drawing is, that red tint is going to show through. You want to be that red tint—the foundation of understanding when it comes to relationships, sex, boundaries and communication. The groundwork you've spent time and effort building is what can help them differentiate between Godly relationships and boundaries and worldly relationships and boundaries.

They have the ability to understand respect, mutual desire and the importance of boundaries. God has entrusted you with this and you have everything it takes to instill moral, compassionate values within their precious little minds. It's far harder to create a new foundation when we're trying to erase all the nonsense those *oh so experienced* 4th graders mentioned to our kids before we got the chance. You want to be the one to set the foundation. God's description of the sacred subject is what you want your child to anchor back to when they hear about people who have lots of boyfriends or girlfriends at the same time. If they can anchor to a biblical standard, when they're inevitably exposed to pornographic images or videos, they'll immediately recognize the sin and corruption. They'll see that pornography illustrates unhealthy and uncommitted relationships, inequality, lack of respect and very often violence against women. There should be a mutual desire, respect and agreeance whenever any sexual activity, including holding hands, hugging or kissing, takes place. While 3rd-5th grade seems early to mention pornography, my experience working with kids tells me we should be teaching them about *good pictures vs bad pictures* in 1st or 2nd grade.

> *Hebrews 6:19-20 (NIV)*
> *We have this hope as an anchor for the soul, firm and secure. It enters the inner sanctuary behind the curtain, where our forerunner, Jesus, has entered on our behalf. He has become a high priest forever, in the order of Melchizedek.*

We need to be the first to reach them. Don't rely on those little knuckle heads (obviously other people's kids, not yours) to teach your kids about sex in its sacred, biblical context because they're going to fall short. Don't wait for other kids to teach your kid about their unconditional value. God's plan is so much greater, so much more fulfilling and creates a wholeness within our spirits that the hookup culture could never provide. Where can you start these discussions when they're in 3rd-5th grade? Discuss healthy relationships.

Healthy Relationships

If a couple disagrees on stuff, does that mean it's an unhealthy relationship? What makes a relationship unhealthy or healthy? What are healthy privacy boundaries in a relationship? What does trust look like in a healthy relationship? Keep in mind, relationship can refer to friendships, familial relationships and also romantic relationships. With how much stuff we see just on TV commercials, it opens the door for some fantastic conversations. Make an extra effort to watch TV with your children and see what they're watching. Use that as a starting point to discuss whether or not the relationships depicted are healthy. Ask them what they would do if they were ever in those situations. Ask them if things like what you're seeing on TV has ever happened at their own school. Tell them a story or two about when something similar happened when you were in school.

> ### *Genesis 50:20 (NIV)*
> *You intended to harm me, but God intended it for good to accomplish what is now being done, the saving of many lives.*

Genesis 50:20 can be such a great reference for these tough conversations. When the enemy throws something in our path, we can use it as an example to teach our kids what is Godly, how to handle these situations and how to shield ourselves from these situations in the future. I know we want to shelter them from the immorality infecting our society but we also have the responsibility of preparing them for a world without filters. There is a balance. Lucky for you, there are endless opportunities to be a living, breathing example for your babies.

Here are a few ideas if you aren't sure where to start:

Scenario 1: You're leaving the grocery store and the magazine headline says some hot celebrity cheated on their spouse for the 37th time

Parent Response: How sad. Cheating on your husband/wife is unhealthy and will be extremely hard for them to recover from. What people don't realize is that it will be just as damaging for the person who cheated as it will be for the person cheated on. We'll have to pray for them. Why do you think people cheat?

Why? You've shown compassion rather than judgment. You've opened the door to get in their heads. Do they think cheating in a relationship is normal? If they listen to mainstream music, then yes, they might.

Remember to "fight the urge!" We want to listen, listen, listen. Try not to be the one to break the silence in between statements. It's far more effective to guide the kid into the right answer by asking questions than to combat their statement.

Scenario 2: You're sitting at home and a Victoria Secret commercial comes on TV.

Parent Response: (calmly) Nope. *changes channel* Not up in here. It'd be pretty awkward to watch a commercial like that if Jesus was sitting right here on the couch with us, huh? If something is coming on TV that we know we shouldn't watch, we change the channel, even when we're grown ups.

Why? Now they know how to create their own filter. Great preparation for a world without filters is to regularly show them the ways you avoid temptation. This also creates the possibility for deeper discussion about guarding our hearts and minds. We can't control the actions of others and we can't control our initial thought, but we can always choose how we'll respond and what our 2nd thought will be. Lastly, if the conversation gets rolling, it's important to ensure they know Jesus loves the half-naked Victoria Secret models just as much as he loves girls who don't dress that way. God is love. He is always love, regardless of our actions or behavior (1 Corinthians 10:13).

Scenario 3: You're picking your 5th grader up from school. They're talking about how one of their friends has a girlfriend who doesn't let him have female friends.

Parent Response: What do you think about that? Is telling someone not to have friends a healthy or unhealthy trait of a relationship? Why do you think that?

Why? Now we're getting them thinking about what boundaries in a healthy relationship look like. Kids need to know what healthy and unhealthy relationships look like before finding out by personal experience. If they've thought about it in advance, they'll recognize red flags much earlier.

Can you think of other opportunities you'd have to casually spark a similar conversation?

_____

_____

_____

_____

_____

What's so special about our responses is that we get the opportunity to reflect the love, compassion and grace that Jesus shows us every day. It's easy to be judgmental. It's easy to look down on people. It's easy to point out everything others do wrong. But no matter how many times we fall short, he continues to love us the same and patiently guides us back toward the path of righteousness. What a beautiful love he has for us. He reminds us constantly throughout the bible that His mercy and loving-kindness endure forever. That should be our goal as parents. Yes we will fall short, but we should strive to reflect the mercy and loving-kindness with others that He shows us in every way. Will you do this overnight? Perhaps not. But start today and you will make significant progress.

> ### Esphesians 2:4-10 (NASB)
> But God, who is rich in mercy, because of His great love with which He loved us, even when we were dead in trepasses, made us alive together with Christ **(by grace you have been saved)**, and raised us up together, and made us sit together in the heavenly places in Christ Jesus, that in the ages to come He might show the exceeding riches of His grace in His kindness toward us in Christ Jesus. For by grace you have been saved through faith, and that not of yourselves; **it is the gift of God, not of works**, lest anyone should boast. For we are His workmanship, created in Christ Jesus for good works, which God prepared before hand that we should walk in them.

Masturbation

I could not ever remember what it was called, so I usually called it, "manufacturing." My parents would tell me it was bad to do, but I never for the life of me could understand *why* it was bad. For your children and mine, I'd like to start be reframing this and elaborating. When you go pee and have to shake your penis or wipe your vagina, that is not shameful and you have no reason to feel guilty. I often felt guilty if anything felt different when I wiped myself after going to the bathroom. I felt guilty for sleeping with a pillow between my knees because I thought if the pillow touched anywhere near my vagina, I had sinned. Neither of these things are sinful.

Boys often begin getting erections at a very early age. Sometimes they'll wake up in the morning and they're already erect. It's important for them to know that they don't need to feel guilty for getting erections and that erections aren't automatically considered masturbation. What our kids should know about masturbation is that the private parts of our body are capable of more than tinkling (urinating) and that is why they sometimes feel different, but anything beyond that is meant for marriage. When we start to notice that things feel different when we touch them, that does not make us sinful. Sometimes things feel different when touched because that is how God made your body. You can't control an accidental touch that catches you by surprise—like wiping after going to the bathroom or cleaning yourself when showering. However, if you continue to *physically* inquire about why it feels different, the *action* becomes sinful. It doesn't make the private parts of your body bad, but it is disrespectful to do to yourself. If it has to do with the private parts of our body and it doesn't have to do with going to the bathroom, it's supposed to be done in the context of marriage and only with your spouse.

> *I Corinthians 6:18 (TLB)*
> *That is why I say to run from sex sin. No other sin affects the body as this one does. When you sin this sin it is against your own body.*

Depending on the child, you may have to have this conversation before they reach 3rd grade. Some parents will have this conversation before Kindergarten. It doesn't make the kid bad. Some kids figure out how their body works a little earlier than other kids. If they've already masturbated, they should know to confess it, ask for forgiveness and continue on their path of resistance. Explain to your child that secrets about bodies can do a lot of harm. When we keep touches a secret, even when we are only touching ourselves, it makes us more likely to do it again. Confessing doesn't mean you'll get in trouble.

When a child confesses, we should strongly applaud their bravery and courage and ask them how we can help keep them from doing it again. We want to help keep them aligned with Christ and we, as adults, know better than they do how dangerously powerful temptation can be. You can avoid discussing what orgasms are if they're satisfied with the definition you've provided. The child should know what an orgasm is by the time they reach 5th grade. If they ask questions prior to fifth grade, it is perfectly okay to share this information with them. Remember, God created orgasms and God does not create shameful or dirty things. We don't need to feel bad about teaching our kids about this stuff.

Orgasms are meant to be experienced with your spouse in the context of marriage, and masturbation tempts us to experience an orgasm without being married and without having a spouse. As the children get older, you can help them understand that it leads down a harmful path of temptation and fantasies that set a purely physical expectation for an experience that's meant to be **shared** emotionally, mentally, physically, and spiritually. If we have these experiences regularly prior to marriage, we may struggle to associate why an orgasm, or even sex, would bond us to another human being because we will have had numerous experiences *alone*. This can have a negative effect on marital sex if an individual struggles to bond sexually with his or her spouse. That can take time and a lot of effort to heal and recover from. Fortunately, this is completely avoidable. Avoiding the temptation is key.

Sexual Harassment

This phrase sounds far more intimidating and heavy than its actual definition. When we think about sexual harassment as adults we usually imagine a slimy supervisor making extremely forward advances with their assistant or secretary despite her obvious embarrassment and lack of reciprocation. It's not always that obvious, especially for our 3rd to 5th graders. Sexual Harassment is *any* **unwanted** behavior of a **sexual** nature. That's it. If it's unwanted, that means we don't want it. If it's sexual, that means it has to do with the private parts of our body, our sexual orientation or a sexual topic. Sexual harassment can be verbal, non-verbal (hand or mouth gestures), written or electronic.

If someone snaps your bra strap, it's considered (physical) sexual harassment because your bra holds up a private part of your body. If someone asks you out or hits on you repeatedly it's considered (verbal) sexual harassment because they're trying to pursue you romantically when you've already made it clear that it is unwanted. If it's wanted, then you'll say yes and they don't have a reason to keep asking you out. They fact that you've already said no but they disregard your rejection and continue asking you is what makes it harassment; your "no" means their pursuit is unwanted. If someone catcalls the pitcher during a baseball game, it's considered (again, verbal) sexual harassment because the person catcalling doesn't know whether or not it's wanted. If that is your mutual crush then it's likely they don't mind, but the key is *knowing, not assuming,* whether or not it is wanted. We want to be respectful of the boundaries other people set and give them the opportunity to set them. Our little nuggets (kids) also need to know that they have every right to set their own boundaries. If they've already been empowered to set their own physical boundaries when they're not comfortable hugging or kissing Aunt Marsha, this will be a far easier transition for them. It won't feel as awkward saying what they're comfortable with because they've done it before—probably on more than one occasion.

Especially as our littles transition from 5th into Junior High, we'll begin hearing more and more about the other girls in class that are, "hoes, skanky, or slutty." Written sexual harassment is if someone were to write it down somewhere other than online. Calling someone one of these names online or in a text is considered (electronic) sexual harassment because they certainly don't want to be called that (unwanted) and those names reference sexual topics and sexual activity (sexual in nature). If someone sends an unwanted nude or partially nude photo, that is considered sexual harassment. Even if both kids are willing to exchange nude or partially nude photos, it's important for them to know that is legally considered production and distribution of child pornography because they are under 18. We often want to get mad at the kids who send them, and we are constantly telling kids to avoid sending nude pictures of themselves not only because it's inappropriate but also because it's dangerous. What would the outcome be though if we put just as much emphasis on teaching our kids not to ask, encourage or pressure others for nude photos as we do about telling them not to send them? While the kids seem young to be discussing nude photos, this is unfortunately age-appropriate. I'm on the board at a non-profit organization that presented to over 6,600 kids in the greater Kansas City Metro area in 2017 about social media safety. We do anonymous surveys at the end of each presentation if the school or church gives us permission. Astonishingly, roughly 1/3 of the Junior High and High School students confessed to sending or receiving nude photos with someone they initially met online –or— meeting up in person with someone they initially met online. Parents were horrified to hear it, because they never imagined kids in Junior High would be participating in that behavior.

Unfortunately, there are many parents who dismiss statistics like this and say, "oh *my* kid would never . . . " and that feeds the problem. Our kids need to have these conversations with us. We need to start the conversations.

Good questions for our kids about sexual harassment:

1. **Is holding hands considered sexual harassment?**
2. **Parent Message:** It's only considered sexual harassment if one of the people participating doesn't want to be holding hands. If two people like holding hands, then it isn't sexual harassment, but they need to make sure they both give consent to the hand-holding beforehand. How could someone let their crush know their boundaries around holding hands or kissing?

3. **What if boys are rough-housing and one of them pulls down the other ones pants?**
4. **Parent Message:** It's considered sexual harassment because nobody wants their pants pulled down (unwanted) and it exposes either our underwear, which are associated with the private parts of our body, or it exposes the actual private parts of our body.
5. **Who would you feel comfortable telling if someone called you or a friend a "hoe" online?**
6. **Parent Message:** Reminder of the 5 Person Rule. Our kids, whether 5 years old or 105 years old, should always have 5 safe grown ups they would tell if someone ever made them uncomfortable or tried to see or touch the private parts of their body.
7. **Is telling someone they have a fat butt considered sexual harassment?**
8. **Parent Message:** Assuming they don't want to be called that (unwanted), then yes, because it is referencing the private parts of our bodies. If you just call someone fat, that isn't necessarily considered sexual harassment because it isn't talking about our privates. However, it isn't kind to call someone fat and there's no need for us to comment on other people's bodies. There's many ways commenting on someone else's body can lead downhill (lust, envy, judgment, jealousy) rather than uphill (kindness, grace, righteousness).

What other questions or examples can you think of to discuss with the children in your life?

_____

_____

_____

_____

Biblical References for Tough Situations:

TV Shows, movies, commercials music, language
    (Ephesians 4:29; Ephesians 5:3-8; 1 Peter 2:1,2)
Damage of justification & reasoning
    (Ephesians 4:26-28; James 1:19-21; James 3:5-10)
How we look at and speak about others
    (James 2:14-22; Proverbs 18:21; Galatians 5:13-26)

Godly Roles vs. Minimizing

Parents of boys and girls in America, Canada and every other nation—hear me and hear me well—boys are not an urge with legs. We need to stop making them think that because their hormones rush around like pinball, they have little to no control over their response. There's about 6 billion (exaggeration) ways I can think of this being harmful, but bigger yet, we're giving them the American culture version of who they are instead of teaching them the truth about their identity in Christ. Our society minimizes boys and girls considerably from being who they're called to be as children of God. Intentionally? Nope. But consequences are more influential than intentions.

> ### *Proverbs 18:21 (NIV)*
> *The tongue has the ower of life and death, and those who love it will eat its fruit.*

The "boys will be boys" statement discussed earlier on transitions from someone chasing you on the playground to trivializing or normalizing sexual harassment. As they reach high school or college, they hear about guys who had such intense sexual urges, "they just couldn't contain it anymore" and then ended up sexually assaulting or raping someone. Is that how sexual violence works? Not even remotely close; assault is not about desperation or intense sexual urges, it's about control, power and entitlement. On some level, our boys might begin to wonder if that will ever happen to them because for so long they've been taught they can't control it. Now they might have fear of what their own body will bring them to do. If you know anything about Satan, you know he's going to prey on that fear and do everything in his power to convince them that God must have messed up—their urges are far too strong for their will power. He's a liar.

I think I was in 4th grade when I first heard the phrase, "guys have two heads and they always think with the wrong one." As a young fourth grader, I was confused, but I still managed to understand they were referencing "his boy part." How present is the enemy in that statement? He is such a deceitful manipulator. He's a professional when it comes to attacking areas God created for our good and trying to infiltrate the opinion or perspective we have of it. If he can take our God-given urges and emphasize their strength to a point that we question our ability to control them, we're far more likely to slip into using those urges out of the context which God created for us. There is always a spiritual element to the situations we face in everyday life, including the conversations our kids hear about their potential or their shortcomings.

In the 3rd to 5th grade range, our kids need to hear how much effort and work and detail and precision went into creating them in order to withstand the lies the enemy tells them through others. Our kids will behave based on who they believe they are while in their search for their true identity. As parents, we play a substantial role in forming that visual for them. Our responsibility isn't small, amiright?! God sees a whole bunch in us to have told us to be fruitful and populate the earth and here we are with these little dudes and dudettes that we have to raise up according to HIS image, often while working full time jobs and trying not to starve our families by consistently overcooking the chicken or burning the meatloaf. The first step, though, in teaching our kids about who they are in God's image is recognizing where we've allowed society to influence our own thoughts and behavior. Let's get an encouraging, uplifting word on that whiteboard brain of theirs before Satan tries sweeping in with the deceit that maybe we fell for when we were their age. The truth of the matter is, the skills we have will help us fulfill the purpose God has for our lives. The obstacles we overcome in life will help us in the areas where we can grow, so that when it comes time to be bold in our faith to take one step closer toward His plan, we'll have experiences where we can look back and say, "God had me then. I know he's with me now, too." There will be things along that way that will be hard and that might make us cry and that's okay—God gave us tear ducts for a reason. He created us, both men and women, boys and girls, with emotions and the ability to process difficult situations. We're able to express the things we feel and depending on our age, we may express them in different ways. This is one of many reasons it's important to align ourselves with who we are in Christ and who God created us to be.

Our culture and society will tell boys that they aren't manly if they show emotion or if they cry. Being the head of the household and a leader for your family doesn't mean you can't have emotion. God wouldn't have given boys and men emotions or tear ducts if they weren't supposed to have them. Society will tell girls and women not to be so sensitive, but if they're aligned in Christ, they'll know the level of their sensitivity was determined with precision and careful focus by the one also created the heavens and the earth. Society will tell teens to wear revealing clothing so they can *catch the eye* of their crush, when God calls us to find the one whom our soul loves. Society will constantly tell us that we aren't good enough. We are everything we are meant to be when we align ourselves in Christ. How we see ourselves is completely dependent on the mirror we choose to look into when we wake up every morning; will we choose society's distorted, dishonest mirror that tells us our experiences determine our value, or our true, raw, beautiful, restored, complete mirror that we can only see when we look through the eyes of God?

What have others made you believe about yourself that doesn't align with how God views you?

_____

_____

_____

_____

What have others made you believe about *others* that doesn't align with how God views them?

_____

_____

_____

Ephesians 2:10 (NIV)
For we are God's handiwork, created in Christ Jesus to do good works, which God prepared in advance for us to do."

Romans 8:17 (NIV)
Now if we are children, then we are heirs–heirs of God and co-heirs with Christ. If indeed we share in His sufferings in order that we may also share with His glory."

Micah 6:8 (ESV)
He has told you, O man, what is good; and what does the LORD require of you but to do justice, and to love kindness, and to walk humbly with your God?

> ### *Psalm 37:3 (NKJV)*
> *Trust in the LORD, and do good; Dwell in the land, and feed on His faithfulness.*

This scripture is from Paul to the saints in Ephesus, but when I read this it so powerfully tugs my heart to show me what a parents prayer should be for their children.

> ### *Ephesians 1:17-18 (NIV)*
> *[For I always pray to] the God of our Lord Jesus Christ, the Father of glory, that He may grant you a spirit of wisdom and revelation [of insight into mysteries and secrets] in the [deep and intimate] knowledge of Him. By having the eyes of your heart flooded with light, so that you can know and understand the hope to which He has called you, and how rich is His glorious inheritance in the saints (His set-apart ones).*

6th – 8th Grade: Digging Deeper

Alright parents, don't freak out. We've got to dig a little bit deeper and I may say some things or use some phrases in this chapter that shoot your eyebrows up to your hairline. Unfortunately by this point, everything we're discussing here is actually age-appropriate. They're getting older and hearing so much more from the kids in class, on their sports teams or on the tv shows they're watching. This age range is approximately 11-13 and by this point, our kids have a relatively clear understanding of sex. They'd probably even feel comfortable answering other kids questions. By 6th grade, we know it's very likely someone has tried to show them a pornographic image or video, or perhaps they've stumbled upon one (accidental or not) on their own. By this point, either they or someone they know is playing with those "bases." If you aren't sure what I'm referencing here, a *home run* means to have sex. The bases are code for how *far you go* with someone.

Temptation

If you walk up and slap me in the face, that is going to hurt. Please don't ever do this. It would hurt because when God made us, he put these fancy little nerve endings all throughout our body. My nerve endings letting me know that you slapped me and that it hurt would be a completely normal thing for my body to do. If I walk outside and it's dusty out, I might sneeze. Again, this is totally normal. God was so cool about the way he made us on even the most fundamental level. Well, we also notice things we like and don't like. By 12, your child can probably tell you if they're more into blondes or brunettes, who their celebrity crush is and what their favorite characteristic is on said celebrity crush. This is normal. They need to know that while it's normal to *notice*, we have control over how long we allow ourselves to look.

Noticing there is someone bathing in the river isn't sinful. Hanging out and watching them bathe in the river is definitely sinful and contains a decent amount of lust. You won't watch someone bathe if you don't like what you're seeing—you following me? Or perhaps you're watching out of envy. Also not okay. Having accountability partners we can turn to when we're being tempted is a great way for kids, teens and adults to avoid falling into any of the many traps the enemy tries to set before us. It also allows us an opportunity to be there for other friends when they are being tempted.

An example for a time when your child may need an accountability partner (or accountability team—4 or 5 partners) would be if they are home alone and their crush wants to come over. Perhaps it's Summer Break. Sure, the parents probably wouldn't find out, but the child knows they aren't supposed to have the opposite-sex over if parents aren't home. The child could instead text an accountability partner and see if they want to come over instead, have someone to keep them distracted or ask for ways to turn down the offer.

> ### 1 Corinthians 10:12-13 (NIV)
> *So, if you think you are standing firm, be careful that you don't fall!*
> *No temptation has overtaken you except what is common to mankind.*
> *And God is faithful; he will not let you be tempted beyond what you can bear.*
> *But when you are tempted, he will also provide a way out so that you can endure it.*

As an adult, who are people you could turn to that could be a positive influence on you if *you* were tempted to fall short?

_____

_____

_____

_____

_____

If you happened to think of people you *can't* turn to, let's evaluate what role they're playing in your life. When are you spending time with them? Keeping someone around just because they're funny, have good connections or because they've been in your life for a long time isn't worth the position they put you in by getting you to cuss more, drink more or perhaps get you to let your eyes wander a tad beyond your spouse. Perhaps they joke about the pornographic videos they saw recently. There are people that will bring us closer to God and people that will take us further away from him. They will not do both. After we go back home, we are the ones that have to deal with where we are spiritually. If we're expecting our kids to separate themselves from people they've been calling friends, we need to acknowledge how tough it can be to separate ourselves from someone we enjoy hanging out with. We also need to know what standard we are setting when it comes to the friends we've shown them we've selected. Surround yourself with people willing to nourish you spiritually and encourage your kids to do the same.

> ### *Galatians 5:16-17 (NIV)*
> *So I say, walk by the Spirit, and you will not gratify the desires of the flesh. For the flesh desires what is contrary to the Spirit, and the Spirit what is contrary to the flesh. They are in conflict with each other, so that you are not to do whatever you want.*

Not every youth group is going to bring your child closer to God, but if you can get them in one they really enjoy and in one where the youth group leader makes them feel comfortable asking questions and openly discussing God, you may have found a good spot! Youth groups can offer support from kids that are experiencing the same temptation and struggles. Having friends or mentors they can text or call or even pray with may be the way out they need. I'd also highly recommend asking the youth group about whether or not they'll be discussing purity or sex to make sure they're going to do so in a trauma-sensitive way. You could even ask them to host a sexual violence training prior to going on any trips or retreats. Right now perpetrators are able to get away with more because they think nobody assumes people really do stuff "like that." By requesting a training, you're letting them know that you are familiar with sexual violence and that you want those surrounding the youth group to be familiar with it as well. You simply bringing it up can help put your child in a safer position.

Take Every Thought

If I sit here and watch other people do math problems, I won't magically be able to calculate the problems myself. If I sit here and think really hard about alcohol—how it smells, how it tastes, maybe even how much it costs—I won't be able to feel drunk. It won't matter how long I sit here and try to imagine drinking it. I could sit here and stare directly at a bottle of liquor, but there will be 0% tipsiness because my mind won't respond that way. I could do the same thing with cocaine. No amount of imagination can get me to "think myself" into feeling high. Sexual thoughts are dangerously different.

We strive to teach our kids about purity and keeping themselves "pure" in terms of virginity without acknowledging or discussing the fact that purity is so much bigger than their virginity. There are plenty of people who have their virginities but are not pure. If you're a virgin but are addicted to pornography, are sexting and exchanging nude photos, or even daydream about sexual activity before bed or when you're bored, how can you claim purity? If someone has their virginity but they masterbate, should they be claiming sexual purity? No, probably not. The key is to understand your prayers should never be for God to remove the desires he gave you, rather, it should be for you to manage the passion HE created for you and to enjoy it within the context HE has provided. The context he has provided is within the covenant of marriage. We also need to understand that we'll continue to strive for purity long after we reach the marital milestone. Purity envelopes the heart and mind of a person, not just the presence or absence of their virginity; it is a lifelong effort.

> *Philippians 4:7 (NKJV)*
> *And the peace of God, which surpases all understanding,*
> *will guard your hearts and your minds in Christ Jesus.*

It's our job as parents to **teach our kids to take every thought captive**. Choosing which thoughts we allow to linger and what topics we choose to meditate on are all a part of taking every thought captive. Our thoughts will turn in to our behavior, so controlling our thoughts has more preventative power than we may realize. Matthew 12:33 tells us that a tree is known by its fruit. If you see apples growing on a tree, you'd never wonder if that's an orange tree or a tangerine tree. You know it's an apple tree because there are apples growing on it. Humans are the same way. Input is output and our actions are a reflection of what's taking place in our minds. It is far easier for the man who has sinned in his mind to fall into temptation physically than it will be for the person who chose to run from sinful thoughts. A person who consistently resists temptation mentally will reflect that behaviorally. Someone who internally struggles with sexual fantasies, envy or pride is inevitably going to reflect those thoughts through sinful behavior. Keep in mind, a *child* who's acting out with anger, violence or aggression at school isn't fueled by healthy, happy thoughts; what society would identify as a "troubled child" is in reality a child that is showing adaptive behavior to trauma, familial instability or significant hardship. We know a tree by its fruit and the actions of a person are a reflection of their internal state.

Matthew 12:33 (NIV)
Make a tree good and its fruit will be good, or make a tree bad and its fruit will be bad, for a tree is recognized by its fruit.

2 Corinthians 10:3-5 (NIV)
For though we live in the world, we do not wage war as the world does. The weapons we fight with are not the weapons of the world. On the contrary, they have divine power to demolish strongholds. We demolish arguments and every pretension that sets itself up against the knowledge of God, and we take captive every thought to make it obedient to Christ.

There are probably countless things you'd never want anyone to know you've thought (I know that's true for me), but Jesus pities us and pours mercy down repeatedly. There are also many stories in the bible we can turn to and witness other people who had negative thoughts or questioned God's ability to get them out of the situations they faced. We question and reason and try to use logic instead of faith. Let's make a cognitive effort to choose simple faith in place of the questioning, arguing, debating and reasoning we use against God when trials come our way. Our children need to see what it looks like to leave the problems we face in God's hands. It is thoughts reminding us of God's Word, His promises and the truth that are going to fuel a pure life. It will give our children a foundation for keeping a positive mentality when adversity throws a stick in their path. The scripture Mark 8: 12-21 should give us all comfort if we are the type to reason instead of step out in faith. Even the people who had seen Jesus perform miracles before their very own eyes struggled with reasoning over faith! I encourage you to read through these verses and ask yourself what areas of your life make you feel (sometimes, or frequently) like your problem is a bigger obstacle that what God can (or will) mend.

> ### *Mark 8:12-21 (NIV)*
> *He sighed deeply and said, "Why does this generation ask for a sign? Truly I tell you, no sign will be given to it." Then he left them, got back into the boat and crossed to the other side. The Yeast of the Pharisees and Herod The disciples had forgotten to bring bread, except for one loaf they had with them in the boat. "Be careful," Jesus warned them. "Watch out for the yeast of the Pharisees and that of Herod." They discussed this with one another and said, "It is because we have no bread." Aware of their discussion, Jesus asked them: "Why are you talking about having no bread? Do you still not see or understand? Are your hearts hardened? Do you have eyes but fail to see, and ears but fail to hear? And don't you remember? When I broke the five loaves for the five thousand, how many basketfuls of pieces did you pick up?"*
>
> *"Twelve," they replied. "And when I broke the seven loaves for the four thousand, how many basketfuls of pieces did you pick up?" They answered, "Seven." He said to them, "Do you still not understand?"*

Take a moment to reflect on Mark 8:12-21. Share your thoughts below.

_____

_____

_____

_____

If we as adults struggle to keep every thought rooted in a hopeful, faith-filled position, we can only imagine how tough the same would be to do as children. What are a few areas of your life where you can make an extra effort to take every thought captive and demand a positive outcome, seeking and expecting God to show up for you?

_____

_____

_____

_____

What are some areas in your life where you do a good job at leaving it in God's hands?

_____

_____

_____

_____

Falling Short

Every last one of us has fallen short. We all have a yesterday. If you think about how many people you smooched before your wedding day, you might have to count on your fingers, your toes and even your spouse's fingers and toes to name them all! I'm not here to bash you for it. Even if you did a bit more than *smooch*. It's because of our yesterday that we want so badly to pour into our little ones. We've been there already. We know what can make them feel whole and what can make them feel regret. We know what manipulation looks like. We know what embarrassment looks like. We know what love feels like. We want them to know what true love is and to wait to have sex until they can experience it in the context for which God created it.

Satan has tricked parents into incorporating fear and shame into the sex talk for YEARS. He's convincingly whispered into parents' ears, "Don't talk about grace when you teach your kid about sex or then they're just going to go do it! If you teach them that they'll be forgiven, they're going to go lose their virginity!" or maybe he said something like, "Tell them all the bad stuff that can happen with it to make it sound less appealing! Tell them about Chlamydia! Gonorrhea! HPV! Oh and AIDS! Don't forget AIDS! Herpes...Oh, and Zika can be transmitted with sex! Tell them about Zika! If they're afraid of sex they'll never want to do it! Tell them they'll get pregnant and then their whole life will be ruined forever!"

Meanwhile, Satan is whispering to the child, "Your parents don't want to be honest with you. They're trying to hold you back from having fun. You're not going to get gonorrhea, that stuff probably doesn't even exist anymore. If it was so bad, nobody would be doing it. People *are* doing it and people like it. Your parents are only telling you the bad stuff." He plays us against each other. Not anymore, yall! God is reclaiming the sex he created us to have and in the context he created us to have it. We have to give sex back to God because for far too long, the enemy has used it to influence, manipulate, shame and control us. We deserve to enjoy the spirit fulfilling, flaw-embracing, loving, vulnerable, marital sex that God planned for us and part of that means ensuring our kids understand its context. We deserve to understand that if and when we fall short, even if it's not going *all the way*, grace is there to catch us and bring us back up again.

> ***1 John 1:9 (NIV)***
> *If we confess our sins, he is faithful and just and will forgive us our sins and purify us from all unrighteousness.*

By being honest with our kids about marital sex being great, we're taking away opportunities for Satan to drive a wedge of distrust between us and our little ones. We have to teach kids about grace when it comes to sex because even if they don't fall short enough to have sex, they can feel guilty enough that they may be tempted to throw in the towel and go further than they otherwise would have. While we, of course, want to tell our kids about the potential consequences of sex, we don't want consequences to be the "meat and potatoes" of what we're telling them. We also don't want them to think their value is dependent on their virginity, because not an ounce, not a fraction, of that is biblical. I can't tell you how many Christian survivors have admitted that after they experienced child sexual abuse, they figured there was no reason to keep from being sexually active because they were already dirty. It's a perspective that asks, "If I no longer have my virginity, who is going to want me?" Our kids can retain the same "oh well, might as well" mentality even if the sexual experiences they had weren't abuse. Maybe they just let things go a little too far with a boyfriend or girlfriend. Regardless, kids deserve to know that every single shortcoming, every potential transgression whether in their past or in their future, whether or not it is sexual, will 100% of the time fall under the umbrella of things that God can forgive us for. This is so much bigger about whether or not they're going to let their boyfriend or girlfriend make out with them in the back row at the movie theatre.

Do we want them to do that? Absolutely not. That stresses me out just thinking about it. But I can't allow my fears to stand in the way of my daughter understanding what it means to have a heavenly father who loves her so unconditionally, beyond any ability to earn more love through good works or good deeds. God loving us enough to create something that not only honors him but is something we would enjoy so, so much is the meat and potatoes of the conversation.

Our kids should know these very basic things:

- Sex is great in the context of marriage, where it can be experienced with sacrificial vulnerability and the comfort of "forever." A nice illustration of vulnerability is in Genesis 2:25. It's a great way to get your kids to think about what it means to be mutually vulnerable with a spouse.
- Sex is pure and wholesome because God made it for a husband and wife. There is nothing dirty about that. (Again, Gen. 2:25 is awesome)
- Sex can be a lot for people to handle because it is a physical, mental, emotional and spiritual act, *simultaneously*. There is a high level of maturity necessary to experience it in its entirety.
- If we experience sexual things outside of marriage, that can leave our hearts hurting and it will require us to find emotional and spiritual healing before having marital sexual experiences and sometimes even needing to continue healing during our marriage. Healing is possible, but avoiding sexual experiences before having them with our spouse can save us from a lot of unnecessary hurt and work.
- Sex is one way that infections can be transmitted, and the chances of those infections being transmitted through pre-marital sex is more common that with marital sex because there will be more people *crossing paths* with each other

- Sex is how babies are made and that is one of the blessings that comes from having sex. It can be really scary to get pregnant outside of marriage because raising babies alone is hard.
- Babies are meant to come after a marital commitment where two people are dedicated to raising a child together.
- Sex was created by God and God creates some pretty awesome things. Sex is no exception.
- There is nothing you can ever do to make God love you less and nothing you can ever do to make him love you more. Sex is no exception.
- Even if you slip up and have sexual experiences before you're married, God will forgive you and he wants to help bless the rest of your path up until marriage. He allows U-turns and he wants you to do your very best to stay in alignment with His word. He will help you heal. The whole point of him wanting you to wait until you're married is because he doesn't want you to have to go through the hurt of bonding with someone on that deep of a level and then experiencing the hurt of that person not being your soulmate. The best way to know if that person is going to be your soulmate is to see if you two end up getting married. Waiting stinks, I know, but it's so worth it.
- You will never be tempted by anything that you don't have the strength to reject or an opportunity to get away from. God promises to give you a way out of every tempting situation. Praying will help you stay focused on him and it will also help you avoid tempting situations.
- This is often taught incorrectly, but the truth is that **God will never *tempt* you**. God would never try to make you fail or fall further away from Him (James 1:13).

Kids deserve to know who God truly is and who they are in him. I trust that God has given my husband and I everything we need to show our daughter who he is. I trust that God has given you everything you need to teach your kids who he is, as well. Satan's lies have convinced parents that the best way to teach kids about sex is to highlight all the harmful things that come from experiencing sex outside of God's plan, rather than teaching kids how wonderful sex is within God's plan. While the grace topic can be intimidating when it comes to sex, we have to first recognize this truth: we grow in our desire to do what is pleasing to God when we recognize how undeserving we are of His love and mercy and how freely and generously He is willing to shower us with it anyway. When we feel His grace and experience his presence despite all we've done wrong, he has an opportunity to show us that despite all the bad we've reflected upon, he still wants us.

Those experiences change hearts and make us seek out what HIS will is for our lives. We aim to please him and do what he calls us to do because we recognize the unfailing, unwavering, never-ending love that we breathe in everyday as if it were oxygen, even though we are completely undeserving! That is what will make your child want to seek His will. There is a calling for each person on this planet, your child included.

> *Psalm 103:10-13 (NIV)*
>
> *He does not treat us as our sins deserve or repay us according to our iniquities. For as high as the heavens are above the earth, so great is His love for those who fear him; as far as the east is from the west, so far has he removed our transgressions from us As a father has compassion on His children, so the LORD has compassion on those who fear him;*

What might be hardest for you or your spouse when it comes to teaching your kids about grace is facing a buried memory of something you haven't forgiven yourself for. Talking about stuff that's challenging often makes our mind play tricks on us and we then think about other things from our past experiences that were challenging. Perhaps it's even something you haven't accepted Jesus' forgiveness for, although you may have asked for His forgiveness many times. He forgives you. Guilt and shame are not of God. If you feel guilt and shame, that is the enemy trying to hold you back and keep you defeated. Satan will create a stronghold so you'll remain crushed in spirit, ashamed to seek God and to make you feel undeserving of love from those around you. God wants you to be encouraged (II Thes 2:16-17). Accept His forgiveness and then choose to forgive yourself; no matter how terrible it was. A lie many of us have fallen for can be broken by reading Psalm 103. Whether our sin was addiction or murder, drunkenness or promiscuity, "as far as the east is from the west, so far has he removed our transgressions from us" (Psalm 103:12). We are not our sin. We are not our shortcoming. This can be a powerful tool for healing after experiencing abuse, too, because survivors often internalize the shame and guilt that was never theirs to carry in the first place. No matter what we have experienced or what has happened to us, no matter what we've done to others, that does not change who we were created to be. That is a lie of the enemy and we are justified in understanding, claiming, accepting and receiving the shame-drowning grace that Jesus provided us when he died upon the cross. Our identity is in Christ and Christ alone (1 John 5:19).

> ### *Isaiah 54:9-13 (NIV)*
> *To me this is like the days of Noah, when I swore that the waters of Noah would never again cover the earth. So now I have sworn not to be angry with you, never to rebuke you again. Though the mountains be shaken and the hills be removed, yet my unfailing love for you will not be shaken nor my covenant of peace be removed," says the LORD, who has compassion on you. Afflicted city, lashed by storms and not comforted, I will rebuild you with stones of turquoise, your foundations with lapis lazuli. I will make your battlements of rubies, your gates of sparkling jewels, and all your walls of precious stones. All your children will be taught by the LORD, and great will be their peace.*

How could a love like that create anything for us that wasn't the top-of-the-line, absolute best?

Honesty is Hard

Can we all agree that sometimes kids ask ridiculous questions that we don't know how to answer? When your kid busts out a, "Did you have sex with dad before you guys got married?" or a, "Why is my birthday only 1 month after your wedding anniversary?" then welcome to the uncomfortable territory of feeling like honesty is stupid. I laugh thinking back to elementary school and all the nonsense I asked my mom. Mom, thank you so much for not sprinting out of the room when I was asking about things far beyond what was age-appropriate. You and dad always made me feel like I could come to you with anything, and you reinforced it enough that I came to you with a little bit of everything. We had some of the most awkward and uncomfortable conversations but you made me feel safe coming back, so thank you.

My mom picked me up one day after school in Elementary. I hop in the car just clueless to the fact that what I'm about to say is likely to swerve our car straight into a ditch. Quirky and unassuming, I buckle my seatbelt as I say, "Hey mom, what's a blow job?" I can only imagine the curse words that flew threw her head and she doesn't even cuss! Someone needs to send that woman an Oscar. Maintaining her composure, she put on a deliberate, award-deserving, *thinking* face. "Hmm . . . a *blow job*?" followed by a long pause. She tried so hard not to whisper that word as she said it so I wouldn't know something was up. She began driving us away just as she usually would.

Then, avoiding a horrifying conversation about oral sex or why anyone would do it, "I have no idea what that is" came out. I believed her, but the question didn't go away. Certain I'd just remembered the phrase incorrectly, I began thinking outloud,

"Bbbllllow job? Plow job? No . . . I think it's blow job." Whether or not a blow job was a real thing never crossed my mind. I knew it was real and I was pretty certain it was something sexual. She ends up saying, "Sorry mija (we're Mexican and that's an endearing nickname in Spanish), I don't know what it is." As far as my momma knew, I dropped it. But, nope. Being the resourceful child that I was, I asked my neighbor. Yes, you read that right. I asked my neighbor.

She was always my go-to if my parents didn't answer my questions with the detail I wanted. She'd give me all the wise answers a 13-year-old had to offer and then I'd go back and tell my disappointed mom what I learned. My mom would get very upset, go talk to *friend*'s mom, they'd agree that *friend* wasn't going to teach me things about bodies anymore and then every 8-10 months we'd have the same discussion. Looking back, I can't help but wonder if maybe my parents knew I'd end up asking the neighbor things (again) and then they didn't have to try to figure out how to bring it up. They always tried really hard to make sure I understood they would always be available for me, but I do think they struggled with how to bring up sex-related things if I wasn't the one to bring it to their attention. But, who doesn't?

A few traumatizing things I "taught" my poor mom included anal sex, the definition of lesbian, blow job and a drawing which explained that a boy part has this *bag thing* under it and the bag grows hair. I learned all of these things while attending two private elementary schools and one public school. We had many of these conversations before I even reached 5th grade. Whenever I'd ask the neighbor girl questions about the things I'd heard at school—or *teach* her the things I'd learned—I knew in advance that I was going to end up telling my mom about it and that I'd get in trouble for asking those questions to anyone other than my parents. I also knew that my punishment would be not getting to hang out with her for a long time.

Planning accordingly, I asked as many questions as possible. I managed to learn a lot in short periods of time. Then we'd both get grounded. Neighbor friend who has not been named, I apologize. If you're reading this, please know I'm sorry for getting you grounded all those times and for putting you in such an uncomfortable position. But on the flipside, thank you from the very bottom of my heart for making me feel comfortable coming to you.

There are some things we can learn from this situation:

- **If you don't answer their question, that doesn't make them stop wondering.** Having a plan in advance for what you will say when your kids ask you certain questions is the easiest way to mentally prepare. You don't need to memorize a script, but be ready to at least start with, "I'm so glad you asked me! Thank you so much for coming to me!" because that will be a real game changer for them. They know more than you think, so know that when you make them comfortable, the questions might start pouring out. Welcome them. Know that it's perfectly acceptable to whisper, "I'll give you the answer but let's wait until after your little sister isn't around" or "thanks so much for asking me! I'll tell you on the ride home so people don't hear what we're talking about here at church!" and throw in a little giggle. You can also ask your spouse if he/she knows what the phrase is if you actually don't know what it is. This does not mean you tell them you'll answer *later* and then you never get back to them. Keep your word and tell them when you say you will. Answering their questions doesn't mean you have to go into all the vigorous detail a high school anatomy teacher would provide. Some kids want more details than others and your child may settle for minimal information. If a 4th grader says, "Hey mom, what's a blow job?" an appropriate answer (if you *haven't* yet discussed oral sex) would be, "Honey, I am SO glad you asked me that! A blow job is something a husband and wife might do to physically express that they're in love. It might sound kind of silly, but a blow job is when someone puts their mouth on a penis." Allow them to respond and voice their disgust. Once they're done with questions, very casually throw in a, "I know it sounds gross, but I am so glad you asked me so I could tell you the truth. Conversations like this are meant for kids to ask their parents.

You did the right thing by asking me. Great job. Say, where'd you hear that word anyway?" If you've already discussed oral sex with your child, you can say, "I'm so glad you asked me! It's kind of silly but that's actually a slang term for oral sex done to a man. It makes me really proud that you feel so comfortable asking me questions like this. That's how it should be."

- The reason I felt comfortable going to *neighbor girl* is **because she didn't make me feel awkward.** She didn't seem uncomfortable, so I wasn't either. I didn't feel like I was a bad person for being curious. I didn't feel guilt or shame in her response, even when her response included, "You know you should really be asking your parents these questions instead of coming to me." I felt comfortable because I could ask her while we were hanging out, playing video games, swimming, etc. It didn't need to be a formal, uncomfortable, clasp-your-hands-together- and-stare-at-your-feet, type conversation. I knew she'd tell me the truth.

- **Only answer what you're asked.** Some kids ask lots of questions and expect details. Some kids are satisfied with far less. One reason I learned so much from neighbor girl is because she would sometimes tell me more than what I asked. You'll be able to preserve more of your child's naivety by avoiding filling in the gaps between questions. If they aren't realizing there is a correlation, go ahead and leave the conversation where it is. If they seem to be thinking, trying to connect some dots, tell them you're more than happy to answer any other questions they have. By 8 or 9, they should understand how sex works (a penis becomes hard and is put into a vagina), that it feels good, what creates a baby (something called sperm comes out of the penis and it swims really fast trying to find a female partner, an egg, and that sperm is how daddy is 50% of the baby's DNA even though the baby will grow in the mommy) and how a baby ends up in a mommy's uterus.

- It's perfectly acceptable to **set guidelines** surrounding the private parts of our bodies. For example, "Any questions or discussions about the private parts of our bodies are meant for kids to ask their parents. We don't turn to anyone or anything but parents so that we can make sure we are getting an honest answer. This also means we don't get to answer these questions for our friends. We have to tell them to ask a their parent or a safe grown up." If you know your church does a great job talking to kids about sex, let your kid know they are welcome to ask the youth pastor if they ever have a question. Pediatricians can be great to turn to, especially for the kids that want lots of details. Tell your child that if they'd feel more comfortable talking to the pediatrician without you, you won't be mad and you're more than happy to leave the room. Your willingness to leave the room shows them you respect their privacy and their comfort. Notice that this privacy is a previously approved, safe setting where you know what is taking place behind the closed door. This isn't the type of privacy where they can have their boyfriends and girlfriends in their bedrooms with the door shut—*that* type of privacy is unacceptable. Rules around the house are great, too. A friend of mine has a rule that after 8pm, her kids aren't allowed to about anything "deep" which includes political, sexual or philosophical questions. After 8pm, she gets to relax. Find the guidelines that work best for you and your family.

Choose to be honest with your kids when they ask you questions. Keep in mind that God created sex and your answer can contain whether what they're referring to is sex in a biblical context or if it is sex in a sinful context. You get to set the standard for them of what biblical sex is supposed to look like. Need some guidance on biblical sex? Go check out Song of Solomon. Things get intense and you might blush when they discuss tasting the fruit on the trees! The point is, TV, music, movies, magazines and everything in between are going to do their best to teach your child a few damaging things about sex: it's strictly physical, it's casual and can be done with many friends or even one specific friend designated for sexual activity (commonly referred to as a *friend with benefits*), contraception is irrelevant, having multiple partners makes you experienced, experience makes you good in bed and therefore you are lust-worthy. That's a smidge of what we're up against. We need to beat the enemy to the punch by presenting a Godly, bible-based counter argument before our children are ever faced with the worldly version. Let's create the expectation for what sex is supposed to be so when our kids witness something worldly they'll be able to effortlessly recognize that the sexual relationships depicted are not what God created for us.

Consent

Sixth grade is a good time to start really expanding on the consent discussion. In the Toddler-2nd Grade range, kids learn about consent in terms of physical greetings (hugs, kisses, handshakes). In the 3rd to 5th grade range, kids learn about consent in terms of sexual harassment. If sexual harassment is any unwanted behavior of a sexual nature, we know that we don't have the person's consent because the action is unwanted. In 6th grade, we'll discuss consent in terms of sexual violence and even begin to introduce the role (if any) that modesty plays in consent. While we could introduce this sooner, it's best to save for later because there is more critical thinking surrounding modesty.

Perhaps one day I'll write a book strictly on modesty, because there is certainly far too much to say to condense into a few paragraphs. For now, we'll discuss it in terms of consent. If you've never heard of the term "victim blaming," it's when people place full or partial blame on the victim of a crime for contributing to the crime in some way. If we begin wondering what the victim could have done differently to avoid having the crime take place, we are participating in victim blaming. One of the most common ways we see this play out today is when people ask what a girl was wearing when she was raped. Victim blaming is often founded in the societal misconception that people sexually assault others because of their *overwhelming sexual urges* or sexual desires rather than what actually drives sexual violence—control, entitlement and power. We know sexual desire is not why people sexually violate others, and we know that what a person is wearing can in no way turn another person into a rapist. "But doesn't it make them a target for rape?!" is what many people ask when I give presentations. That question (like many others) is rooted in the idea that people sexually assault others based on sexual desire. Wearing revealing clothing does not make someone a target, because that isn't what drives a rapist's desire to rape in the first place. It's always tough for people to process and understand this because it reveals how susceptible all humans, regardless of clothing, are to being a victim. If rape had to do with sexual urges or desire, statistics on sexual violence taking place against elderly people (in their homes committed by family members or in nursing homes committed by non-family members) wouldn't be nearly as high as they are.

Unfortunately, victim blaming is common because society feeds a false narrative surrounding sexual violence and the people who grow up hearing the victim blaming accept it as truth. Where we see this damage children in the church is that we teach them girls who *respect themselves* (or dress modestly) are less likely to have *those things* happen to them. We'll ask what the girl was wearing when raped as a way of trying to understand what caused someone to commit this crime against her. This also invokes the idea that girls who don't dress modestly are more likely to be, or more deserving of, being sexually violated. Not only is it statistically far from true, but it also takes the focus off the fact that sexual violence is preventable and nobody deserves to be sexually violated. This "immodest people are more likely to get sexually assaulted" idea produces significant self-blame in the survivors who hear these misconceptions used as facts. Whether we have daughters or sons, we need to make sure they all understand that regardless of what anyone is wearing or what "message" we *think* they're sending through their attire, they are still a human child of God that has a voice and a right to say "yes" or "no" without being pressured to say otherwise. We want them to understand that nobody is deserving of sexual violence and that we are morally, legally and ethically required to respect the boundaries people set.

Would God want us dressing modestly? Of course! He created our bodies with sagacious detail and magnificent focus. He knit us together in the womb (Psalm 139:13-16). When I imagine a little grandma knitting, well, first of all, she's in a rocking chair. Her head is slightly tilted and she's a little bit plump. Her attention to detail is effortless, but she's strategic and graceful with every move she makes. That's what a *human* does when knitting a blanket or a scarf. My mind can't even process the gravity and symbolism behind knitting together a central nervous system, strands of DNA or a thumb print. How did He mold and shape our bones, tendons and joints? How incredible is our God? We're His masterpiece, and for many of us, there is a special counterpart masterpiece in our future spouse (Ephesians 2:10). There is something beautiful about embracing mystery until you find the spouse you want to share all your secrets with in the safe space of marriage. There are parts of ourselves we can choose to set aside only for the person we're vowing to spend forever with. But, to ensure we're teaching our kids not to look down on others or judge people, it's important they understand that while God would looooove for every single one of us to dress modestly and wait to have sex until marriage, he also wouldn't look at someone disobeying His word and love them any less than He loves the modestly dressed people. Our clothing, appetite, preference in music or level of intelligence does not determine God's love for us. We cannot earn His love and we cannot do anything to make Him stop loving us. This will teach them not only more about God's love but it will also show them how to act like Him, too.

Our kids should also know that while saving all of those things for our spouse is very special, if there is verbal, physical or sexual assault within the marriage, the thought of not wanting to divorce or remarry is no reason to remain in a relationship that is harming you or your children. Safety is a top priority and you belong to God—anyone harming you or treating you as if you are anything other than a child of God is not withholding the responsibility our Lord placed on them when he called the two of you to marry.

Here are my brief tidbits on modesty before I end up writing a Guide to Modesty:

- Dressing modestly is a way that you can honor the body that God created just for you.
- Dressing modestly can give you a special confidence as you enter marriage knowing you're going to share something with your spouse that you haven't shown anyone else.
- Modesty is far deeper than clothing. Modesty is also about the manner in which a person behaves. Since we are called to be like Him, that means we too should value people equally regardless of their level of modesty, level of confidence or level of Christianity.
- Modesty does not make someone more valuable or more worthy of love than someone who is immodest. God loves all humans the same and we cannot earn more love by obeying His Word.
- Teaching kids modesty means "talking up" modesty, not putting down people who don't dress modestly or asking our kids, "What message do you think *she's* sending with those short shorts?" Clothes don't send messages. *Assuming the intention* behind clothing does not determine the actual intention. People have voices, intentions and emotions and are fully capable of speaking whatever message they want received.

If only there were goggles we could hand to our children that would give them the eyes of God, enabling them to see others the way that God sees them. If only it were that easy. If it were, we'd probably need a pair for ourselves, too. Instead, we have the powerful Word of God that can encourage and direct us and teach us how to view the situations we face.

Another thing we can talk about with our 6th graders is consent. They should know a person can't truly consent if there is blackmail, threats, fear or intoxication involved. This is because consent is when someone gives their *willing* permission for something. If I offer to let you drive my car for a day or two and then you blackmail me with something I did in the past, I might be willing to let you drive it longer than I otherwise would have because of the blackmail. That isn't willing permission. If you threaten me, it isn't willing permission because I'm only saying, "yes" based on the threat. A person also can't consent if they're unconscious or asleep. While we can gently touch on intoxication in 6th, we'll dive in much deeper with the drinking once they're in 8th.

What are some situations in everyday life that you can start incorporating the topic of consent?

_____

_____

_____

_____

The key is to empower our children to realize they have say and responsibility for the body God gave them. They are our babies, and they'll always be our babies, but God has His own mission and will for their lives. They are here to increase His Kingdom in the ways that God has planned for them. That part can be hard for parents to remember. We like to claim them as our own, but they belong to God. Our job is to raise them up according to His word, love them, encourage them, and guide them as they prepare to step into the purpose he has for them. While we can clearly set boundaries like, "no tattoos or piercings on YOUR body while you live in MY house or rely on MY income," we also want them to know how to say "yes" or "no" to things relating to their body long before they're out on their own.

8th Grade: Consent & Intoxication

There is a prison-letter in the book of Philemon that so simply yet profoundly explains the meaning of consent. If you're not familiar with this one-chapter book, it is about a runaway slave named Onesimus. Let me start by saying I do not endorse slavery nor do I think it is a good thing. There is, however, a lot that can be learned from this story. Onesimus runs away from Philemon where he ends up not only crossing paths with Paul (who is now old and in Prison) but also surrendering his life to Jesus Christ. They became close and bond over their mutual love for God. Paul would love to enjoy the last of his days sharing the gospel with Onesimus, but he wants Philemon to permit it. Paul writes this letter for Onesimus to take back and present to Philemon so that he will be not only be forgiven for running away, but will also be treated no longer as a slave but as a brother in Christ (Philemon 1:16). Paul basically butters Philemon up for the first 9 verses of his letter and then, becoming vulnerable, shares that sending Onesimus back to Philemon is like sending his very own heart (Philemon 1:12). What I find so funny about this is that Paul openly states that he'd really like to keep him! He then states, "but without your consent I did not want to do anything, so that your goodness would not be, in effect, by compulsion but of your own free will" (NASB).

Had Paul kept Onesimus instead of sending him back to Philemon, it wouldn't matter how willing Philemon would have been to gratify Paul, he'd have had no opportunity to truly express or illustrate that gratitude if he hadn't sent Onesimus back. (3. http://biblehub.com/philemon/1-14.htm) Paul's essentially saying, "Look, I'm just going to put the ball in your court. I really, really want to keep Onesi with me to share the gospel together, but I didn't know if you would be okay with that. To make sure you were 100% cool with it, and to make sure you would make the decision that was truly in your heart (rather than being pressured to let him stay with me since he's already here) I'm sending him back to you for you to make that decision."

Similarly, when it comes to sexual consent, we want to make sure that even if it's just a kiss, the person we are kissing isn't kissing us out of feeling pressured, guilted into it, forced or even feeling like they should do it just because that's the most convenient option right now; we want the person to be genuinely, consciously, whole-heartedly, willing. They should want to kiss us, not just agree to do it cause we want them to.

We want the decision to be made so that if there were no external pressures, that would be the decision they would want to make anyway. Being intoxicated, either by alcohol, drugs or prescription medication, makes it extremely difficult to determine whether or not that person would have made the same decision had they not been intoxicated. Being like Paul, we want to leave the ball in their court. When it comes to being intoxicated, sometimes alcohol and drugs make you do things you otherwise wouldn't have done. The only way we'll know with complete certainty if the person would have willingly consented is to wait until they are no longer intoxicated. Yes, this may be more inconvenient, but it was also far more inconvenient for Paul to send Onesimus back to Philemon. He did so anyway, though, because he wanted to make sure that Philemon was making the decision willingly. Paul wanted his consent.

Let's pretend Onesimus went and presented Philemon with the letter, but Philemon was actually asleep when Onesimus held it up. Onesimus could say, "Welp, the Phil man didn't say anything so I guess I can go back to Paul!" Right? Well, yes, he could technically do that, but he certainly wouldn't have Philemon's consent. Sleeping people don't give consent. Neither do unconscious people. We are looking for an enthusiastic, "yes" from clear-minded individuals.

What we want our kids to know is this: if you respect someone and love someone enough to have sex with them, then respect them enough to wait for them to be in a completely clear state of mind before participating in any sexual activities. It doesn't matter if the two of you have done it before and it doesn't matter if they got drunk willingly. If they wanted to do it and it had nothing to do with being intoxicated, they would do it sober, too.

High School: I've been there, Honey

If you weren't already stressed enough, here comes the driver's license, prom and varsity football games. Fortunately, God isn't worried about it. He doesn't want you to worry about it either. By this point, your relational and educational foundation is set and now we simply reinforce it. This means while your stress might be higher, you actually have less materials to teach and more opportunities to listen. They know all the anatomical stuff, they understand how sperm and eggs create babies and they know that orgasms are meant to be experienced in marriage. It may take a good amount of energy to listen as they tell you about the things going on with *other students* at school, but keep in mind that they may be telling you those stories about the *other kids* in school just to see the way you respond. If you always keep your cool, they're going to share far more with you than they would if you say something like, "Taylor did what?! Wow. Her mom would be so hurt and disappointed." While it's likely that Taylor's mom would indeed be hurt and disappointed, you've got a much better shot at keeping the communication open if you respond with, "Poor Taylor. She's in a really rough position. Does she feel comfortable talking to anyone about it? She needs someone she feels safe talking to."

Lines of Communication

In this stage there are only two big things you need to work on: keep the door of communication open and reaffirm your child's identity in Christ. What might surprise you when I mention this door of communication is that I don't only mean with you. In high school especially, your child should have accountability partners who he or she can rely on in times of temptation or weakness. Your child should also have an up-to-date version of the 5 Person Rule. Perhaps the people your child felt comfortable coming to when they were 10 or 12 years old, they don't have the same relationship with now that they're 15.

Maybe a volleyball or baseball coach has come into their life and booted someone else off the list. Regardless, having that extra layer of support can help keep them on the straight and narrow. It's also a good idea to have extra support because let's face it—it doesn't matter how good of a parent you are—in those high school years, your kids probably don't like you that much. Not because you've done anything wrong, but because they're yearning for independence and you're that final roadblock keeping them from it.

So how can we help them? While hiding them in the basement and not letting them be around the opposite sex sounds like the easiest option, it's unrealistic and probably illegal. Realistically, it does not matter how much you try to guard your child or keep them from being in situations where they can do any freaky-deaky stuff, there will be an opportunity where they have to make a tough decision on their own. We want to ensure that they've been given all the Godly tools to win that spiritual battle. It may seem like a physical decision, but their spirit being aligned with God's word will be what enables them to overcome the temptation. In a way, we should really be grateful that it's a spiritual decision, because the decision-making center of a human brain doesn't fully develop until around 25 years old. (https://www.urmc.rochester.edu/encyclopedia/content.aspx?ContentTypeID=1&ContentID=3051)

One of the most difficult aspects of the high school stage is giving them age-appropriate freedom so they have opportunities to begin making decisions on their own with the parts of their brain that *are* developed. We can look back on our own high school years and remember the times our parents weren't there to make the decisions for us; let's keep in mind the times we made the right decisions and use that to shape our kids into being responsible, hard-working, God-seeking adults. Their safety is still a top priority and biblical standards will always be in play; age-appropriate freedom doesn't mean overstepping either of those safeguards.

What are some opportunities your child may have to make a decision on their own?

_____

_____

_____

If the **5 Person Rule** never mattered before, it certainly matters now. You're under-appreciated and they're over-confident in their understanding of life. They may feel comfortable coming to you with questions about dating, but if something happened where they thought your feelings would be hurt or that you'd be disappointed, they may be inclined to talk to someone else instead. Even if it isn't always us that they are coming to, our kids need to have 5 safe adults they'd feel comfortable talking to if anyone ever pressured them, made them feel uncomfortable or tried to touch them when they didn't want to be touched.

Who has your child/children selected as their updated 5 safe grown ups?

1. _____

2. _____

3. _____

4. _____

5. _____

Beyond the 5 Person Rule, there are some tools we can use to keep those lines of communication open. Teens can use these to play their part in staying safe while they enjoy gaining age-appropriate independence. These can still be applied long after high school, but it's best to begin when there are parents to help oversee and guide the process.

Code Talk

A great way to build on to the 5 Person Rule is to ask who they'd call if they were ever in a situation and they wanted out immediately. The Code Talk people will not necessarily be the same as the people on their 5 safe grown-ups list, but they can be. The Code Talk means having a code word and a location that they could text, and the Code Talk person will know the text meant the teen is uncomfortable and wants to be picked up as soon as possible.

For example, they're on a date and the person is making them feel uncomfortable. The child could then text, "Nunchucks—Chipotle on McDowell Rd." so the adult knew where to come get them. While you can absolutely be one of the people on that list, it's best for them to have a few options. Our goal is their safety. If that means calling Aunt Gina instead of us, so be it. If they're at a party and something happens where they want to leave, they can text, "Hot Cheetos- 123 E. 7th St." There should also be a code word or phrase meaning, "immediate danger, call 911." My husband and I have an emergency code word that we can use anytime, including in person, so the other person knows if we are in a dangerous situation. As you're picking the words or phrases for these situations, be sure it is something easy to remember but not something likely to come up in conversation.

The 4-1-1

Anytime I was going to go on a date, my parents wanted to know where we were going, who all was going and what time I was going to be home. Something my college roommate, Kristin, and I incorporated was to give each other all the details for worst possible scenarios. I'd tell her everything about who I was going to go out with—the neighborhood where he lived, where he worked, who his friends were, who his ex-girlfriends were, height and brief physical description (or a link to their social media) and a time for her to expect me home. We laughed about it and joked that we were being crazy, but it was nice to feel like someone was there with a full description who could call the police if I didn't come home when I said I would. Having a friend to share those over-the-top details can help the teenager feel like they're slowly gaining more range on their *leash* while also doing their part to stay safe.

Telling your parent that stuff means you have to acknowledge how dangerous the world is, and as a teenager, you spend more time trying to convince them that the world isn't dangerous and that, "everything will be fine, *mom*." Having them begin incorporating the 4-1-1 into their routine is also helpful so they're already accustomed to doing so when they go off to college or move out of your house.

Options Following Assault

If we talk to our children about this type of trauma for no other reason but to prepare them to be great advocates when those around them face tough situations, so be it. We need to make sure they know what options a person has after a sexual assault has taken place. A survivor can do a few, all or none of these. It's far more likely that a person will be assaulted by someone they know than a stranger, so these discussions will typically be referring to relationships, friends, friends of the family or even authoritative figures like teaches, coaches or pastors. By having these conversations we're increasing the likelihood that the child will feel comfortable reaching out for help and support.

1. **Hospital:** Reach out to local hospitals and ask if they collect evidence after a sexual assault has taken place. Know what hospitals in the area do and which do not. This is far easier to know in advance than to make these phone calls after being in a traumatized state of mind.

What are 3 hospitals in your area that provide SANE exams? (Sexual Assault Nurse Exam)

_____

_____

_____

2. **Crisis Line:** There are various anonymous, 24/7 hotline numbers a survivor can call immediately after, or long after experiencing assault or abuse. They can call to process the situation and have support as they determine what to do, or they can call to ask questions about what the reporting process looks like. People on the crisis line are trained to handle these situations and answer the tough questions.

3. **Police:** If someone wants to report the crime to police, they can call law enforcement for the area where the crime took place. If you live in Washington but the crime took place in Albuquerque, New Mexico, you'd have to call the police in Albuquerque. They will assign a detective to investigate the situation after you share with them what has taken place.

4. **Therapy:** Sometimes having someone available to talk through all of the emotions that follow assault can help restore the pieces that feel broken inside. A sur-

vivor, and even the family of the survivor, can sometimes receive free therapy depending on local crisis center.

Name two local crisis centers that offer therapy to survivors of sexual violence:

_____Is it free? _____

_____Is it free? _____

Identity in Christ

On a spiritual level, high school is finally where we get to discuss God on a deeper level and really dig into what it means for us to be created in His image. Sure, we get to have decent conversations throughout junior high, but high school is when, as my dad says, "It gets real." I say this with all sincerity—if there is anything that is going to increase the likelihood of your child waiting to have sex until they are married it will be them having a thorough comprehension of the value and grace God sees and has when he looks at them. Can you even imagine what that looks like? Knowing every area of life where you've fallen short, how incredible is it to know that when God sees you, he is proud and excited to see you turn and pursue him despite how many times you've turned away.

This can be helpful to hear for all the teens that have already lost their virginity, too. In a 2012 informative report by the National Campaign to Prevent Teen and Unplanned Pregnancy that surveyed 1200 high school seniors, more than three-quarters of senior girls and boys responded saying that they would change the way their first sexual experience occurred and many responding expressed having mixed feelings about the first time they had sex. Interestingly, seniors in this study wanted their younger peers to know it was, "fine to be a virgin" when they graduated from high school. (http://pediatrics.aappublications.org/content/138/2/e20161348#ref-11)

How powerful would it be if those 1200 seniors and their younger peers knew they were still accepted in the eyes of God and that not all hope was lost? How many of their younger peers could be positively influenced by an honest, open discussion about how caving to peer pressure wouldn't be worth it? How special would it be for them to know their value hadn't diminished and there was no need to *throw in the towel*? We want teens to know that if they've already lost their virginity, **there is still value in holding off until marriage.**

When we associate our value with the things we achieve, we're constantly fighting to achieve more, gain more and earn more. If our value and identity is associated with status, then as soon as we're no longer able to claim the worldly identity of "Virgin," "Starting Quarterback" or "Student Council Treasurer," we feel lost and worthless. How many teens partake in hypersexuality after losing their virginity? Too many. How many people associate value and identity with their looks, so as they begin to age, hundreds and thousands are spent on skin care products, botox, plastic surgery and calorie-deficient diets? Too many. How many athletes fall into a deep depression once they're no longer playing sports at the high school or collegiate level? A lot. After claiming that identity for years, it makes sense why they don't know who they are beneath the jersey. But that was never their *identity* to claim—it was only a stage.

You are not what you *do* or what you achieve. However, if your child identifies himself or herself as a masterpiece, as a complete, restored, chosen child of God, their confidence and view on life won't vary or waver based on whether or not they're named MVP of the basketball team, make Honor Roll or get to be in marching band for a big university. They are entitled to claim that identity because that is who they are through Jesus. A girlfriend breaking up with them, failing their Science test or their favorite show being discontinued won't carry near the weight as it would if they weren't associating their worth with what the world tells them is important.

Their confidence will be shaped according to who God is and not according to their shortfalls or worldly achievements.

How powerful to be able to counter every wordly lie with a biblical truth. We must show our children how to do this. When Satan tells you that you're not strong enough to overcome the obstacles life throws your way, you can say, "It is written, no weapon formed against me will prosper." When Satan says you don't have the self-control to wait to have sex until marriage, you can respond with, "It is written, nothing will be able to tempt me that God won't give me a way out from." That is how Jesus responded whenever Satan or people tried to tempt him. He knew he was the son of God and he approached life accordingly. We've all sinned far more than Jesus ever did, for he was free of sin and blameless, but when he died on the cross, everything you've ever done was nailed up there with him. Every sin, every shortfall, every hurt was placed under the blood of Jesus and because of him we are made whole. They put nails through His feet for all the places we'd go that we never should have entertained. Maybe for you, that place was a strip club or the bedroom of an ex-lover. They put nails through His hands for all the things we'd touch that we knew we shouldn't be touching. They spit in his face and punched him in the mouth for all the wrong words you and I, and our children, would ever say. I know I've said and done enough to send me straight into a fiery pit—but Jesus. They put a crown of thorns over His head for all the things we'd ever think about or look at, that we knew was turning our back on who He's called us to be. The blood of Jesus is powerful enough that no matter the drugs we've done, the porn we've watched, the pre-marital sex we've had, the friends or family we've betrayed—we are restored. I say this with never-ending appreciation and overwhelming gratitude, because I've surely done them all. NOW GET THIS. Because of Jesus, when God looks down on us, he sees us the way he sees Jesus. How wild is that? He looks at us, despite all of our sin, and knows we've been made flawless. He sees children that he loves overwhelmingly, that he is fully committed to helping grow in their relationship with him through the Holy Spirit. We are beloved because of who God is, not because of our sin-free past, our good deeds or our ability to overachieve in comparison to our classmates, siblings or coworkers. He wants to help us stay on track and he's there, at our fingertips, all around us. He's given us His Word so that we have a complete manual on what to do when we face trials, tribulations, divorce, assault, wrongful persecution, temptation and everything else in between.

Do your kids understand that grace and love can't be earned by good behavior, volunteer work or doing their best to live a sin-free life?

Understanding our identity in Christ isn't something we can hear once and then fully comprehend. It takes meditating on scripture and silent time with God. "So how is my child going to choose to *meditate in scripture* when you already told me they basically only have half a brain until they're 25?!" is something you might be thinking right now. Realistically, they probably won't be meditating much...*unless they see you do it.* We have to show our kids what that looks like. How we handle situations, how we talk about ourselves, how we talk about God and how we talk about others are all a great start. Talking isn't enough, though. Our behavior has to reflect the Godly things we say. Our behavior and our words that *aren't* Godly often come from the things TV, social media and unrealistic societal standards set for us. Helping our children to identify in Him instead of identifying in celebrities, music and tv shows will give them courage to separate themselves from cultural norms. Your child hanging out with like-minded individuals will help to pour life into them and keep them strong in the Lord. Having the support of friends who help us know God, the less we care about what the people around us are thinking of us. Does God think less of you if you didn't lose those last 30 pounds after having a baby? No. Does God think less of you if you could never grow burly, manly facial hair the way your dad did? No. Does God think less of you if you are absolutely terrible at sports no matter how much effort you make? No. You are everything God wanted you to be when he formed you in your mother's womb. He wanted you to be your exact frame and your exact height. Your nose isn't too big and your eyes aren't too close together. If your hair was supposed to be blonde he would have given you blonde hair. You are perfect and blameless and chosen and restored.

When we align our identity, worth and value with who God is, our view of life and circumstances change profoundly and we're able to rise above situations. We are everything he ever wanted us to be. Think about your life and encourage your kids to think about their own lives, and recognize that you are all consecrated, redeemed and learning to walk in the fullness of all that Christ is in you.

Part of teaching our kids about finding their identity in Christ means teaching them that God's love doesn't change depending on whether or not they wait to have sex til marriage, kill someone or become addicted to gambling. Acknowledging the unconditional mercy and grace of God's love is in no way an endorsement for sin or bad behavior, but it's wildly irresponsible for parents to overlook grace based on a fear that the child will take it as permission to act out. Our kids will not hear that God is going to love them no matter what and decide that it's a green light to do as they please. Hearing words from the Father speaks to the soul, not just to the physical mind.

> ## *2 Cor. 1:21-22 (NIV)*
> *We learn that when we were born again, God set His seal of ownership on us and put His Spirit in our heart guaranteeing what is to come. Since then it's God Himself who makes us stand firm in Christ. Having freed us from the one who held us in slavery, He set His own seal of ownership on us. We are no longer slaves but sons and daughters of God. Having been bought at a price, the precious blood of Jesus, we belong to God now, and no one can ever change that.*

What do you believe God sees when he looks at you...honestly?

_____

_____

_____

_____

> ### *2 Corinthians 5:14-19 (NIV)*
> *For Christ's love compels us, because we are convinced that one died for all, and therefore all died. And he died for all, that those who live should no longer live for themselves but for him who died for them and was raised again. So from now on we regard no one from a worldly point of view. Though we once regarded Christ in this way, we do so no longer. Therefore, if anyone is in Christ, the new creation has come: The old has gone, the new is here! All this is from God, who reconciled us to himself through Christ and gave us the ministry of reconciliation: that God was reconciling the world to himself in Christ, not counting people's sins against them. And he has committed to us the message of reconciliation.*

> ### *Titus 3:4-7 (NIV)*
> *But when the kindness and love of God our Savior appeared, he saved us, not because of righteous things we had done, but because of His mercy. He saved us through the washing of rebirth and renewal by the Holy Spirit, whom he poured out on us generously through Jesus Christ our Savior, so that, having been justified by His grace, we might become heirs having the hope of eternal life.*

We're soaked in grace and mercy on a daily basis. What makes it twice as overwhelming is that God longs to be gracious to us (Isaiah 30:18, NIV). We don't earn it by volunteering in a soup kitchen or by driving grandma to her doctor's appointment for the 37th time this month. We minimize the glory of God's grace by trying to convince ourselves that we could do anything on this earth to earn His love. Rather, understanding that he will never walk away from us, no matter how far off track we get will sustain us if we take the time to process it. It takes really sitting and chewing on that scripture (Titus 3:4-7) to even begin to grasp what that means for us. Have you ever been in a situation where you looked up and realized this was absolutely not the destination you were planning for, but when you look up, Jesus is right there walking with you. It doesn't matter how far you sprint away from His glorious plan for your life, He will always be with you.

When is a time in your life that you got off track and Jesus didn't leave your side?

_____

_____

_____

_____

If you can't think of anything, you feel free to give me a call. You can borrow a few of my stories. I've got more than enough to go around. For others, perhaps this is a moment that you're realizing you've never accepted God's forgiveness or you still wonder if he's forgiven you. I don't need to know what you got into to tell you that he never left your side, he loves you unconditionally and there is nothing about you that he views as tarnished, worn down, *used up* or troubled. If you've asked for forgiveness, God has separated you from your transgressions as far as the east is from the west (Psalm 103:12). If you've asked for forgiveness, God has tossed it so far away from you it might as well be buried at the bottom of the ocean (Micah 7:19).

> ### *Micah 7:19 (NIV)*
> *He will again have compassion on us, and will subdue our iniquities.*
> *You will cast all our sins into the depths of the sea.*
>
> ### *Isaish 1:18 (NIV)*
> *Says that God will make our, "scarlet sins as white as wool."*
>
> ### *Psalm 103:12 (NIV)*
> *Expresses the thought in yet another way: "As far as the east is from the west, so far has He removed our transgressions from us."*

It's terrifying for many parents to tell their kids that God will love them regardless of the decisions they make, but it's our job to pour His Word out onto them so they'll understand His desire for our lives and the reason behind those desires. We're scared because Satan is telling us we need to be. The Lord does not give us a spirit of fear (2 Timothy 1:7), and we have to stand firm in Him so the enemy will not sway our duty to teach our children what the Word of God says. I believe God and I believe His Word is good. His Word doesn't teach me that sex is dirty or shameful, so I'm going to do everything in my power to teach my daughter (and any future children I have) all about it without any of the things Satan and his manipulation try to tack on to it.

> ### 1 Peter 3:3-4 (NIV)
> *Your beauty should not come from outward adornment, such as elaborate hairstyles and the wearing of gold jewelry or fine clothes. Rather, it should be that of your inner self, the unfading beauty of a gentle and quiet spirit, which is of great worth in God's sight.*
>
> ### Psalm 139:14 (NIV)
> *I am fearfully, wonderfully, and purposefully made.*
>
> ### Colossians 3:1-3 (NIV)
> *I am in Christ, and nothing can change that.*
>
> ### 1 Corinthians 6:20 (NIV)
> *The goal of my body is not attraction from others, but worship of God.*
>
> ### 1 John 4:9-11 (NIV)
> *I am loved completely.*
>
> ### Psalm 90:14 (NIV)
> *Wholeness is found when I'm satisfied in God.*

I highly encourage you to open your Bible and read through the scriptures where God shows us who we are in Him. Take your time. Sit and chew on the scripture and keep notes of what it means to you each time you review it. Ask God to reveal to you what He wants you to see not only for your children, but also for your own relationship with Christ.

Handling Disclosures

As we talk to our kids about their bodies and boundaries, we create an environment where they can come to us with questions, comments or concerns. Sometimes, as we create this trust, they may disclose that someone has violated a boundary they have set. Perhaps it isn't even our own child that is disclosing sensitive information. Regardless, our response in these situations is crucial to their healing and self-confidence. It's critical that we respond in a way that reinforces comfort and safety, so they don't regret the moment of vulnerability. We also don't want them to receive a negative response from us and then recant out of fear. There is so much going through a child's mind when they're debating whether or not to disclose abuse, including that they often love the abuser (because it's typically an acquaintance or family member) and they don't want to get them in trouble (https://www.rainn.org/statistics/children-and-teens).

This can sometimes lead to kids being so loyal to the abuser that parents find out by the child unintentionally "slipping" information. Being able to identify an accidental disclosure and reciprocating with positive reinforcement (being grateful for trusting us, praise for the bravery it took to tell someone and reassurance that they did the right thing) can also be the defining moment in whether or not that child will be able to accept help. Parents won't reach out for services to fix something they aren't aware happened; accidental disclosures provide just as much opportunity for healing as purposeful disclosures, so long as they're handled appropriately.

Responding Appropriately

The first person a survivor tells is the one who will have the biggest influence on their healing. If the first person a survivor tells begins yelling or crying, it doesn't matter if every single person following that experience does a great job, the survivor will have a far harder time healing than someone who had a positive initial disclosing experience. They may actually apologize and say it didn't happen just to make the crying or yelling stop. Responding appropriately means responding in a calm and collected manner and letting the child know we believe them. This may mean needing to take slow, deep breaths or counting to 10 with 1 slow inhale and exhale in between each number. There are a number of ways we can do this, but one thing more likely to help us handle these situations than thinking on-the-spot is to have a plan in place for what we'd say if a child (whether our own or someone else's) were to ever disclose they've experienced sexual abuse.

Appropriate initial responses:

- "I believe you, I'm so sorry this happened and I want you to know it wasn't your fault."
- "I'm so sorry that happened, honey. I believe you. Thank you for telling me."
- "It wasn't your fault and I believe you. I'm so sorry. I'm glad you felt comfortable sharing with me."
- "May I give you a hug?"
- "Thank you so much for telling me."
- "You didn't deserve that. I'm so sorry. I appreciate you telling me."
- "It was so brave for you to tell me. I bet that was hard to tell someone. I believe you."

- "You have so much courage! There are lots of kids who would have kept this a secret, but touches should never be secrets. Thank you so much for telling me."

Ideal response:

"Thank you so much for telling me. I'm so sorry that happened, sugar pie. I believe you. I bet it was really hard for you to tell me this. I want you to know that it wasn't your fault and that you're not in any trouble. You are so brave for sharing this with me. Thank you so much for telling me" – allow a pause for them to respond.

You may even witness them feel relief in your response by their physical (body language) response. If you hear them sigh, see their shoulders relax or their hands become unclenched, these are each signs of relaxation and relief. If after a period of silence they don't share anything else you can say, "Is there anything else you want me to know?" If not, bring the conversation to a close and maybe get them a snack or turn on a show they like. The ideal closing would be, "Well, sweetie pie, I want to do whatever I can to keep you safe. I'm going to have to tell a safe grown up who handles situations like these to make sure that this doesn't happen to you or any other little kiddos again. Do you want to tell them instead or would you rather I do it?" The child will almost always respond with wanting you to do it instead, but the fact that you're giving them a choice makes them feel empowered. We want to help them get their choice back. We want to then immediately report the abuse.

In those emotional moments it's easy to want to cry or scream or ask many questions. It is of vital importance that we remain calm and composed. In the mind of a child, if you respond irrationally or with significant sadness, anger or questioning, now the child thinks they've made you upset and they are far less likely to ever open up about it again. Their mind is saying, "If you are a grown up and what I've said is making you *this* upset, it must be really bad and I definitely can't talk about this again. I did something really bad." Furthermore, it's important to remember how confusing it is for a child to be in this situation as they typically love the abuser. It's important not to talk badly about the person for two reasons: we don't want the child to shut down and we don't want to confuse the child even more for having positive feelings toward the person who caused them harm.

When you want to say horrible things about the person, consider instead:

- "Sometimes people we like a whole bunch end up doing things that hurt us. Not everyone who we like or love will hurt us, but even if someone only hurts us one time, we want them to know they aren't allowed to hurt *anyone* at all. Not even once."
- "Sometimes good people do bad things. That can be really confusing for us. Do you know what the word 'confusing' means?"
- "When people do things that hurt our feelings or make us feel weird, sometimes we need to spend some time apart to figure out how to feel about the situation. Spending time apart can help us a lot."
- "It's okay to pray for people who do bad things just like we pray for people who do good things. We want to ask Jesus to help change their heart so they don't try to hurt people anymore. It's also okay to be mad at those people for hurting us."
- "Part of healing means getting help. The people who do bad things to hurt other people need to get help so they don't hurt people anymore and people who have been hurt sometimes have to get help so they can heal and not feel sad about things that have happened to them."

Regardless of what they say or who they say did these things to them, we want to be careful not to ask many questions because a child's mind doesn't process information the way an adult mind processes information. We could actually contaminate their memory of the event by asking questions in the wrong way or asking questions in a way that makes them think we want to hear a specific answer. For example, if you ask a 4 year old, "When did this happen?" they might respond with, "In the morning." That might not mean it happened *this* morning. It might have happened 6 months ago but it happened *in the morning* 6 months ago. These are things that a children's detective would understand and be able to navigate far more effectively than a non-professional. Our job as parents is to remain calm, believe our kids, have compassion and do what we can from this point forward to keep them safe and support them. Let's leave the questioning for the detectives.

Reporting Abuse

Many parents will hear their child disclose abuse but then refuse to report it because "if the child is making it up, we could ruin that person's life." Sometimes they'll also refuse to report because the person accused is a very close friend, a pastor at our church or even a family member. A situation often seen is when the abuser is an older step-sibling or cousin. All of these situations should absolutely be reported, including if it is another child acting out sexually. It is likely that the child who is acting out sexually is doing so because they are currently experiencing, or have previously experienced, their own abuse. By reporting the child is having sexual behavioral issues does not sentence them to a future of condemnation and doesn't label them as an inevitable rapist—they are not inevitably a rapist. By reporting a child is acting out, we could be doing our part to put an end to whatever trauma they are experiencing and help them bring healing from something they've experienced in the past. Detectives see many of these situations. They want both perpetrators and victims to receive the help they need to find healing.

When you report that your child has disclosed something to you, what you are basically saying is, "My child told me 'x' and I need a professional to look into the situation." You are not accusing anyone of anything. You are admitting that you are not a child sex crimes professional and that you would like someone who is a professional to determine whether or not they feel the disclosure has merit. One thing I will tell you after spending years in anti-sexual violence world is that kids do not make up child sexual abuse. If they can describe sexual acts or sexual topics it's because they have been exposed to it. Exposing a child to pornographic images or exposing oneself to a child is child sexual abuse. Back to reporting—the person you call will ask you exactly what the child told you and will ask you questions about the person the child mentioned (if they mentioned anyone specifically). There are different protocols for different states, but you can expect that a detective will want to speak to the child directly at the station. When it comes to kids, interviewing them on film (that can later be used in court) is far better than having to go back and repeatedly ask the same questions. Asking questions about the abuse someone has experienced can re-traumatize them whether they are children or adults. Feel free to ask the person you are reporting to as many questions as you need to feel comfortable, including when the detective would want to speak to the child and whether or not you're allowed to be present. If they ask you whether or not you'd like to have an advocate, I'd encourage you to accept and be sure to include your child in the decision. There are court appointed special advocates and often even advocates through local rape crisis centers, but it is up to the person receiving services (or their parent if the person receiving services is underage) to make the decision as to whether or not they want them. Advocacy is a multifaceted position that can benefit survivors in significant ways. Not only are advocates able to provide emotional support and answer questions about the system, but they're also familiar with trauma-informed responses and community resources. A trauma-informed response means when someone's responses in a conversation are based on a deeper understanding on the trauma that the person has experienced. Understanding the way trauma impacts the human brain and what common responses to trauma look like in children or adults makes an advocate that much better. Advocates are able to provide short and long term assistance and are the only part of the system whose entire role is to be focused on the child and you. So while advocates are known for being great listeners and educated on how the system typically operates, the depth of their position is far deeper than what's referenced along the surface.

In summary, we have to stay calm. We want to avoid asking questions and we want to make sure the child who has disclosed knows that we believe them, it wasn't their fault and that we are very grateful they were willing to share it with us. We want to acknowledge it must have been tough and that it was very brave of them to tell us what happened. We want to report the abuse immediately. After reporting, we can check out what resources are available nearby for the child to begin age-appropriate therapy like play therapy or art therapy. If you are unfamiliar with either, definitely look into them. Since children don't always have the vocabulary to express themselves, they're able to use other forms of expression and creativity to find healing. We, as parents, may also consider seeing a therapist; the hurt we internalize when something happens to our children is profound. It is absolutely warranted to seek therapy after finding out your child has experienced trauma. There are actually rape crisis centers (depending on where you live) that may offer free therapy to not only the victim of the trauma but also to the family of the victim.

> ### *Psalm 34: 17-19*
> *The righteous cry out, and the LORD hears them; he delivers them from all their troubles. The LORD is close to the brokenhearted and saves those who are crushed in spirit. The righteous person may have many troubles, but the LORD delivers him from them all.*

Author's Notes: Application

These are the examples, models and guidelines the Lord our God directed me to teach you so that you, your children and their children after them may fear (have tremendous respect, adoration and love for) the Lord your God, and His Word, as long as you live. These examples are not the stories of a single child; they are the stories of all of our children faced with trauma. Be sure to listen for God to direct you as you follow this blueprint so that these conversations may go well with you and that you may grow abundantly in a relationship with your sweet children as you raise them up according to the Word (Deut. 6:1-3). For we are God's masterpiece. He has created us anew in Christ Jesus, so we can do the good things He planned for us long ago; teaching our children about the precious creation they are because of the reverence of their creator is no exception (Ephesians 2:10). As a parent, grandparent, pastor, mentor or legal guardian, be sure to remember that all scripture is God-breathed and is useful for teaching, rebuking, correcting and training in righteousness (2 Timothy 3:16). The areas where you struggle in your walk with Christ are not more powerful than the Word He has provided you, for you are of Him, not of this world. Allow it to resonate with your spirit and not only your mind. If it touches your mind but not your spirit, you will walk away from its guidance like someone who looks at his face in a mirror and, after looking at himself, goes away and immediately forgets what he looks like. Someone who looks intently into the perfect law that gives freedom, and continues in it-not forgetting what they have heard, but doing it—they will be blessed in what they do (James 1:23-25). Though you walk this world, you must always remember whose you are. It is the Lord God who formed a man from the dust of the ground and breathed into his nostrils the breath of life—that is how the man became a living being (Genesis 2:7). His breath, His life, is in you. Dads, you have an important role. This culture will do all it can to show your daughters that they're worthy of less while teaching your sons to push and ask for more of someone else's daughter. Be a living, breathing example of what a husband and father is called to be so that your children may see that example and desire it for their own life. Be considerate of how your children view the respect, sacrifice and adoration you show for your wife despite you being the religious leader and head of your household. Moms, you have more to offer than the nurturing, loving, molding affection you use to shape your little ones. You're to exhibit strength and dignity, while looking forward to tomorrow with joy in your heart. Speak with wisdom and faithful instruction not only to your children but to your husband, for you possess spiritual gifts that he may not have, and vise versa. When you begin to age and our society tells you you're less than, hold your head high and remind them that while charm is deceptive and beauty is fleeting, a woman who fears the Lord is to be praised (Proverbs 31:26-31). It will teach your daughters to realize the Biblical standard of their unconditional value and will teach your sons to lead his wife with honor and respect, for she too is an heir for the gracious gift of life (1 Peter 3:7). Finally, all of you, be like-minded, be sympathetic, love one another, be compassionate and humble. Do not repay evil with evil or insult with insult. On the contrary, repay evil with blessing, because to this you were called so that you may inherit a blessing (1 Peter 3:8,9).

With a prayer for blessing,
Geony

Author's Bio

After graduating from Long-Island University/Post Campus with a Bachelor of Arts in Economics, Geony has spent a career in victim advocacy. She serves as a Board Member for KC Street Hope and is President of Value Unconditional, Inc., where she helps people heal from the wounds of yesterday so they can fully experience the gift of today. Her heart belongs to her husband Martin T. Rucker II and their daughter Claire. *Geony's own words capture her mission for advocacy:* "If immediate gratification is possible with community betterment efforts, I have yet to experience it. Working toward the goals I've chosen takes perseverance." You can read more about Geony Rucker at this link: http://inkunder30.com/geony-rucker/

Recommended Reading

The Beginner's Guide to the Gift of Prophecy by Jack Deere

Victory in Spiritual Warfare by Tony Evans

Beauty for Ashes by Joyce Meyer

Insignificant by Apostle Pam Brown

Sources

Internet Resources in order of reference:

1) 1 in 4 girls, 1 in 6 boys ...
   http://nctsn.org/nctsn_assets/pdfs/caring/ChildSexualAbuseFactSheet.pdf
2) 93% of kids know their abuser
   https://www.rainn.org/statistics/children-and-teens
3) Toddlers - Tickling
   http://bigthink.com/robby-berman/why-we-may-love-to-tickle-but-we-mostly-hate-to-be-tickled-ourselves
4) Redirecting to more socially acceptable behavior
   http://wyomentalhealth.org/poc/view_doc.php?type=doc&id=10119&cn=461
5) Normal and abnormal childhood sexual behaviors
   http://nctsn.org/nctsn_assets/pdfs/caring/sexualdevelopmentandbehavior.pdf
6) Paul & Onesimus: http://biblehub.com/philemon/1-14.htm
7) The decision-making center of the brain:
   https://www.urmc.rochester.edu/encyclopedia/content.aspx?ContentTypeID=1&ContentID=3051
8) It's fine to be a virgin:
   https://www.urmc.rochester.edu/encyclopedia/content.aspx?ContentTypeID=1&ContentID=3051
9) Children loving their abuser:
   https://www.rainn.org/statistics/children-and-teens

Text Resource:

Kramer A. 2012. *Girl Talk: What High School Senior Girls Have to Say About Sex, Love, and Relationships.* Washington, DC: The National Campaign to Prevent Teen and Unplanned Pregnancy.